M000107295

Praise for *Sales Mastery*

"*Sales Mastery* is designed to *increase* your sales revenue. I should know—the past 18 months in Chuck's coaching program have yielded this type of result!"

—Randy Baxter, President, Asset Positioning Services

"Sales Coach Chuck really *awakened the salesperson within*. Using the tactics and approaches found in his new book *Sales Mastery*, I have placed my family in a 4,000-square-foot house, purchased a brand new 2011 Mustang GT 5.0, earned my private pilot's license, and, after that, still put money in the bank! Next up is retirement at age 50. Invest in the *Sales Mastery* book and get to work like I did!"

—Matt West, ThomsonReuters

SALES MASTERY

THE SALES BOOK YOUR COMPETITION DOESN'T WANT YOU TO READ

CHUCK BAUER

WILEY

John Wiley & Sons, Inc.

Copyright © 2011 by Attitude Ventures, Inc. All rights reserved.

Published by John Wiley & Sons, Inc., Hoboken, New Jersey.
Published simultaneously in Canada.

No part of this publication may be reproduced, stored in a retrieval system, or transmitted in any form or by any means, electronic, mechanical, photocopying, recording, scanning, or otherwise, except as permitted under Section 107 or 108 of the 1976 United States Copyright Act, without either the prior written permission of the Publisher, or authorization through payment of the appropriate per-copy fee to the Copyright Clearance Center, Inc., 222 Rosewood Drive, Danvers, MA 01923, (978) 750-8400, fax (978) 646-8600, or on the web at www.copyright.com. Requests to the Publisher for permission should be addressed to the Permissions Department, John Wiley & Sons, Inc., 111 River Street, Hoboken, NJ 07030, (201) 748-6011, fax (201) 748-6008, or online at http://www.wiley.com/go/permissions.

Limit of Liability/Disclaimer of Warranty: While the publisher and author have used their best efforts in preparing this book, they make no representations or warranties with respect to the accuracy or completeness of the contents of this book and specifically disclaim any implied warranties of merchantability or fitness for a particular purpose. No warranty may be created or extended by sales representatives or written sales materials. The advice and strategies contained herein may not be suitable for your situation. You should consult with a professional where appropriate. Neither the publisher nor author shall be liable for any loss of profit or any other commercial damages, including but not limited to special, incidental, consequential, or other damages.

For general information on our other products and services or for technical support, please contact our Customer Care Department within the United States at (800) 762-2974, outside the United States at (317) 572-3993 or fax (317) 572-4002.

Wiley also publishes its books in a variety of electronic formats. Some content that appears in print may not be available in electronic books. For more information about Wiley products, visit our web site at www.wiley.com.

Library of Congress Cataloging-in-Publication Data:

Bauer, Chuck, 1958–
  Sales mastery : the sales book your competition doesn't want you to read / Chuck Bauer.
      p. cm.
    ISBN 978-0-470-90019-2 (cloth); ISBN 978-1-118-00784-6 (ebk);
    ISBN 978-1-118-00785-3 (ebk); ISBN 978-1-118-00786-0 (ebk)
    1. Selling.   I. Title.
    HF5438.25.B38 2011
    658.85—dc22
                                                          2010037970

Printed in the United States of America.

10 9 8 7 6 5 4 3 2 1

To Dorothy . . . may her entrepreneurial and caring spirit live on forever.

A special heartfelt thanks to my staff who exercised extreme patience with me as I wrote this labor of love, not to mention their contributions of time, effort, and knowledge in helping me complete Sales Mastery.

And to all the client companies, business owners, and professional salespeople whom I have had the honor of working with through the years, this book is about you and all because of you!

Contents

Foreword

"We did the right thing. It will improve his business," Dan Foreman, the experienced advertising sales executive, says to his less-experienced boss in the motion picture *In Good Company*. As sales professionals, it is our responsibility to master the sales process so that we can effectively serve our customers' needs and improve their businesses. It is really not too ironic to think that the word *sales* is derived from the Norwegian word *seji*, which means "to serve." If you were to ponder this for a moment, you must ask yourself, how can you serve if you do not know your customers' needs? How can you serve if you are not a master of the sales process? This book will help you master the sales process. To be successful in sales and stay in advance of your competition, you must become proficient in the sales process. That is why you should buy, read, and study this book. Chuck Bauer's *Sales Mastery* will help you master the sales process, and you will find yourself overtaking and staying ahead of the competition.

Keeping ahead of the competition means that you must stand out among the brigade of sales professionals selling to your customer. Your customer is beset with sales advances all day long. How can you stand out and above your competition? Being distinctive is key to being a master of the sales process. This book will help you understand the psychology of the sale, which is crucial to being distinctive in the sales (and marketing) process. It could be said that, of all human interactions, psychology is never more prevalent than in a sales call. In a sales call, the guarded buyer actively deflects the seller's advance (we call them objections). It is here where most sales professionals lose the direction of the call. They are often unable to mentally evaluate the call and survey the intellectual landscape of what is happening in the call and then reengage the customer with a distinctive approach that is more in alignment with the customer's needs. The sales process is dynamic and interactive. It is human. There is a psychological and compelling element that is happening in a sales call. The buyer is unaware of this progressive component because it is natural human behavior. You, as the sales professional, should be aware of this factor because a keen understanding of this is the pathway to successful selling and being sales distinctive. Objections are often referred to as "buying signals" in sales training. You might also venture to say that objections are also moments of opportunity for the sales professional. This is an opportunity for you to be sales distinctive and engage your customer in such a way that you are clearly setting yourself apart from all competitors. Behind the objection lies all the buyer's wants, needs, fears, anxieties, insecurities, and so on. If you, as the sales professional, cannot recognize these emotions and approach the call and engage your customer in such as way as to address these emotions with the appropriate response, you will lose control of the call and the ability to effectively serve your customer. The majority of sales books and training focus on the process and, namely, one component of the process in particular, which can be termed as discovery (listening). Most sales books and trainings today do not address the psychology of the sales call. This book addresses the psychology of the sales call. Don't you want to know what your client is thinking when they respond to your sales approach with an objection? Don't you want to know what drives your customers' objections? How can you consult with your customer if you can't get past objections and get to the root business challenges of your customer? How can you be distinctive?

In summary, this book will help you master your understanding of the sales process, master the psychological component of the sales call, and be more distinctive in your approach to your customer's needs. Ultimately it will help you serve your customers better by giving you the tools to identify all the needs of your customer and how your product and service can effectively address those needs. And as a result you will outsell your competition. Now buy this book, read it, study it, and sell. Do the right thing and improve your customer's business.

BARRY TREXLER
Senior Vice President
ChaseHealthAdvance
www.chasehealthadvance.com

Introduction

True Confessions of a Veteran Salesman

As a sales coach, I educate my clients—salespeople and sales managers, business owners, and corporate executives—that if they want to be successful, they must be *distinctive*. They can't copy others' tactics and approaches, but rather must **create their very own sales presence**. Since I imagine this directive might also apply to an author trying to set himself apart, I will begin my first sales book with a confession: though you are reading my book, I do not refer to myself as an author. I am, first and foremost, a salesman. Yes, I coach other sales professionals now, but my knowledge and counsel isn't based on theory. It is based on the practical application of techniques that I have used for many years, techniques that have consistently produced moneymaking and award-winning results. Regardless of whether you're low on the totem pole or well positioned in the corporate hierarchy, whether you're living from paycheck to paycheck or think you should have gold coins stamped with your profile, whether you work for yourself or work for a Fortune 500 company—*Sales Mastery* has information that you can use to skyrocket your revenues. However, it will work only if you are open-minded and willing to make some changes in your sales techniques.

Let me tell you about one of my clients. Jeff is a powerhouse in the real estate mortgage industry in Dallas, Texas. Now, keep this in mind: the mortgage industry has been failing on a national level over the last several years. We started working together in December 2006. Jeff had consulted previously with two other coaches who specialize in real estate sales. They were popular coaches with books, too. But after a combined total of five years with them, Jeff had *not* increased his income. So my eyebrows were seriously raised.

When we met, Jeff was earning approximately $250,000 a year—definitely not bad. However, like many of my already successful clients, Jeff wanted to expand his business. More important, he wanted to maintain his current income level without having to work 12-hour days. His goal was to enjoy financial success while spending some much-needed time with his family.

Jeff and I powwowed about how he was currently selling, and how the ideas in *Sales Mastery* would help him understand sales psychology, work more efficiently, and improve his sales tactics. We made a lot of changes in the way he was milking his market to gain clients. Fortunately, he was open to change and completely willing to implement new ideas.

The result of our huddle was that in a period of just six months, Jeff's annualized income exploded from $250,000 to more than $385,000. This occurred in only six months—in the *mortgage* industry! Jeff continued to increase his income even as the market was collapsing, and he finally had time to become the family hero and take them on that vacation he'd been planning for years. (That red cape looks good on you, Jeff.)

I don't just coach individual salespeople like Jeff; in fact, many of my clients are large corporations with global interests. For these clients, I perform a rotational and customized sales training, teaching different facets of *Sales Mastery* over the course of several months. I've worked with corporate CEOs one-on-one, and I've coached groups of 20 to 30 salespeople and as many as 200 in ongoing classes and in webinars.

In January 2009, I began a long-term contract with a division of a Fortune 100 company. Though they're top-notch people, they had no focus or discipline as a group. Their attitude was more *can't-do* than *can-do*, so sales tenacity wasn't even on the chart. I worked with the sales director, the floor manager, and all of their salespeople—a total of about 30 individuals. Together, we implemented several of the ideas from *Sales Mastery* and, after only one year, their revenues erupted to a 60 percent growth over the previous year.

My point is this: *Sales Mastery* has something for every salesperson, manager, vice president, or CEO of a small, mid-size, or large company, whether it's public or private, domestic or foreign. The information works for every industry that is engaged in sales in any way—which is by and large every industry, period. Prospects are prospects, and clients or customers will always be clients or customers. They must be professionally persuaded to do business with you. You must make them *want* to do business with you, whether your product sells for one dollar or hundreds of thousands of dollars. **Sales Mastery will equip you to generate more money for you and for your company.**

Still Making the Sale, Still Closing the Deal

My sales techniques don't come from Ivy League business schools; they are not rehashed ideas from some well-known author who spends his time speaking and signing copies of his latest book. My ideas are from someone who is still working in the trenches of selling: *me*.

As a sales coach for more than 20 years, I have been traveling the country consulting salespeople and making the sale right alongside them. Every week, I sit in on different types of live sales presentations. Sometimes I'm at a company that logs between 7,000 and 8,000 phone calls per day. Seated in salespeople's cubicles and with a wireless headset on, I listen to their live conversations with prospects. Before they even start talking, I'm already writing comments on a flip chart, like "Smile!" Is a **mirror on their computer** so that they can check their expression? If a smile is not physically present, it's likely to not be present in their tone of voice, either. Another common piece of advice: "Stand up." Are they slouching in a chair, or standing? Does the conversation begin with the all-too-familiar and unprofessional, "Hey?" Do they have goals posted in their workspace?

I can also be wired into sales calls that are taking place anywhere across the country. In these situations, I e-mail my comments as the conversation is happening. When the call is finished, I send an e-mail summarizing everything that went right in the conversation and specific critiques for improvement.

Other days, I attend face-to-face appointments. Because a large proportion of my clients are in the financial services sector, those meetings are often highly confidential exchanges between a registered financial advisor and an accredited investor. I arrive pressed and polished with my client, whose customers don't mind that I'm there. In fact, most are pleased to know that their advisor has a sales coach—and even occasionally share their opinions with me. I can recall one particular appointment where the salesman just *wouldn't stop talking*. When he finally did come up for air—to take the investor's $2 million check to the accounting department—the customer leaned over and said to me, "You gotta do something with that guy." This must have been the day that hell froze over, because the salesperson still managed to somehow get the deal. Unbelievable. In instances like this, I silently observe the interaction and save my comments for later.

Having the opportunity to observe a range of sales presentations in a wide variety of industries gives me a unique advantage: I get to keep my finger on the pulse of the current sales environment, as well as the needs and wants of prospects in a variety of industries. But really, the industry makes no difference. As I mentioned before, a prospect is a prospect—whether you're selling apples or airplanes. There is opportunity for improvement with every sales call. If you are willing to take my experience in the trenches and apply it to your own sales techniques, then you *will* increase your sales.

However, I must caution you: one of the biggest obstacles standing in the way of most salespeople's enhanced success is their ego. **If you really want to make more money, you've got to stop paying attention to that arrogant voice in your head**—the one that keeps telling you that you know it all, you already make a ton of money, you're too cool, you don't need help, there's no room for improvement, and so on.

I run into many salespeople who have become accustomed to selling one way—and one way only—for years, even decades. You've probably met them, too. They're either older with a little bit of gray around the ears, or they're younger with a few too many diplomas on the wall. Guess what is around their feet? Blocks of concrete. They just will not move, will not change.

Don't be that salesperson. Open your mind to doing things differently, and you'll enjoy better results. Guess what? With the right kind of changes and by utilizing methods that are revealed in this book, you are guaranteed an automatic raise!

When I coach a client on a live sales call, I get responses to my ideas for improvement that fall into two categories. The first is, "Okay, I'll do that next time." The second is, "Well, the reason I did it that way is because . . . ." The second response comes from a salesperson who won't prosper or reach his potential. He's not listening to a word that I say; he's only thinking of ways to deflect what I've told him and make excuses for the habits he's determined to stick with.

However, the salesperson whose response falls into the first category is already on her way to making more money. She is coachable. She doesn't take what I say personally, and she is willing to make changes to her sales process. As a result, she is in for a well-deserved increase.

If you are open and available to new ideas, new tactics, new psychology, and new ways to become more efficient, then I can teach you—and your company—how to make more money. Moreover, you will actually be able to work less because you will be working smarter and more efficiently.

Officer Bauer Becomes Coach Chuck

Every salesperson has the ability to work intelligently and efficiently. Some are born with a knack for doing so, while others need to learn. I had to learn. Surprised? Coach Chuck did not come with natural sales talent. Nope—not even close.

After I graduated from high school, I spent two years working as an emergency medical technician and then moved into law enforcement. I was a police officer for five years, but ultimately I decided that wasn't the right career path for me. Of course, I wasn't quite sure what the right career path *was*, so I ended up at a Nissan car dealership in Albuquerque, New Mexico, through a friend's connection.

I'll never forget my first customer. I was so nervous about talking to the man that I was actually trembling, so I just started reading from one of the Nissan brochures. I'd been hiding behind a gun and a badge for five years—tools that did all the talking for me. I didn't need communication or people skills. As a result, I was terrible on that first attempt at a sale. And, of course, I blew it. Right then and there I made up my mind to learn—quickly—from the top guy.

Finding the true winner at a car dealership is easy. The number-one salesperson is always standing alone and separate from the rest of the pack. At this particular dealership, there were about 20 guys together on one side of the showroom, white sleeves rolled up, smoking cigarettes. On the other side there was Bill Grommes: short, balding, a former firefighter whose office wall was lined with Salesman of the Month plaques. In the world of sales, Bill was what I would now call a F.O.N.—a Freak of Nature. Full of tenacity and discipline, the man did not waste one minute of his day. People were drawn to him before he even spoke a single word.

Part of Bill's attraction was his walk. Every step he took made it clear that he was on a mission; I'm pretty sure that if he ever approached a wall with that walk, the wall would get out of his way. (Over the years, I've met some of the world's best salespeople and they all have that walk.) He was the guy making all the money, the guy with all the happy clients, the guy with all of the referrals. So, my first sales lesson. **Walk like you're on a mission**. Walk like Bill Grommes.

During my first month at the dealership, I focused and soaked in everything else Bill could teach me. Then, over the next five years—with high levels of discipline, tenacity, and implementation—I became that dealership's number-one new car salesperson. During my last three years there, I was ranked among the top 25 of all Nissan salespeople in the United States. Not bad for a guy selling cars in a small market like Albuquerque. Plus, I didn't get a single customer who had simply walked into the showroom. Why? Because my referral base was so huge I didn't need to chase people. They were chasing *me*.

How did I get such a high amount of referrals? It came from my willingness to **try a new idea**. I must have been one of the first car salespeople in the United States to invest in a personal computer. It was an IBM PC Jr. that cost $3,300, and I had to get a loan from the bank to pay for it.

The computer came with IBM DOS and Writing and Filing Assistant, but since I had absolutely no clue how to work the thing, the man I bought it from was kind enough to show me the basics. I began by simply cataloging my customers, and then I came up with crazy ideas for letters that I would send to all of them. The dealer agreed to provide paper, letterhead, envelopes, and postage so I could do my mass mailings. I kept doing this, over and over, and my client base went through the roof. At the time, Albuquerque's population was very low—even counting the jackrabbits out in the desert. Yet I managed to sell 30 to 35 cars in some months.

I made a name for myself that way, and I was soon teaching my methods to other salespeople at the dealership. My speaking career began when I was asked to talk at Nissan's regional sales events. I left Nissan to travel the country pitching The Peoples' Network, a satellite television network that offered personal development programming 24 hours a day, seven days a week. I was on the road for three years, hitting two cities each week and typically speaking to audiences of 50 to 100 people. Then, 17 years ago, I started my sales training company in Dallas. There have been many stops and starts and well over a million miles logged while traveling to more than 200 cities.

Along the way I've had the privilege of working with hundreds of eager clients. *Sales Mastery* is not only my book; it's theirs, too. Every person I've coached has adapted these ideas for increasing sales to fit their own particular industry or sales cycle. My clients across the country are constantly finding new ways to improve upon the ideas in *Sales Mastery*. That information funnels back to me, I pass it along to my other clients—and we all prosper. So the question you must ask yourself is not "Will this work?" but rather **"Am I willing to implement *Sales Mastery* and *make it work* for me and my industry?"**

This book is a fully ripened fruit, rooted from the live sales calls that I sit in on each week and the sales training workshops that I conduct around the country. Each chapter includes information from a specific workshop, real-life examples that demonstrate the efficacy of the sales techniques described in the chapter, "Quick Tips" for easy referencing, and a Review Quiz to help you plan how you will use the chapter's information.

Now let me ask you the same question I ask those who attend my workshops: "Are you serious, or are you just kidding around?" **Successful salespeople are either fully engaged or they are completely disengaged.** It's all or nothing. If you're fully engaged, and if you are open-minded and willing to make changes to your sales techniques, then we can begin. My goals are set, my commitment is strong, and my dedication to you is sincere. The content found in *Sales Mastery* will advance you personally as well as professionally.

Godspeed and Good Selling,
Chuck Bauer

1

Sales Distinctions and Success Traits

The most distinctive and savvy salesperson I've ever known happens to be a man who sells insurance in central Texas. When we met, he had been in the industry for only five years and already had become one of the top insurance salespeople in the United States. His schedule goes something like this: he schedules three appointments a day for four days a week, does charity work on the fifth day, and takes off on the weekends. He meets with 12 people during his four-day workweek—a schedule that, over the past five years, has helped him develop an astounding database of 2,000 clients, all of whom have purchased insurance from him. His business is solely referral-based; he has never paid for any advertising or bought a list of leads.

How does he do it? With a uniquely bold sales distinction: he sends a limousine for his prospects or customers and brings them back to his office for a two-hour meeting. If they're hungry, his cook prepares a meal for them. He closes the deal on their insurance options and then sends them right back home in a limo. His clients ride and dine in the lap of luxury. Word about this celebrity-level treatment from an insurance salesman in Texas spread like wildfire. That's all it took for his business to explode.

One more thing: he treats his top clients—about 20 people total—to yet another limousine ride. At the end of the year, they are chauffeured to Dallas for a gourmet meal in a fine restaurant, and then they enjoy a theatrical production of *A Christmas Carol*.

Instead of buying ads or spending money on search engine optimization, this sales professional chose one very special and extremely distinct sales tactic—a tactic that became his weapon of mass revenue production.

That's what sales distinctions can do for you. Figure out what *you* can do to *set yourself apart from the sales pack*—and then *do it*. **Don't overthink the think. Over*do* the do.** In other words, don't overanalyze an idea. Get out of your self-imposed box, and get rid of the ego. Decide what you want to *do* to distinguish yourself, and then make every effort to get it done to the best of your ability. According to the dictionary, distinction is "the act of distinguishing or the condition of being dissimilar, different, or distinct." According to Sales Coach Chuck, distinction is the key to increasing your sales revenue and boosting your sales career. As I say to many of my students, "In sales, you had better become *distinct* or you will become *extinct*!" To reach the top, you *must* leave the beaten path. If everyone else is doing it—whatever "it" happens to be at the moment—then *stop* doing it yourself. Instead, find a different approach, a better way, a technique unlike the others. For example, I recently met a car salesman who wears a black tuxedo—complete with bow tie, studs, and patent leather shoes—whenever he delivers a car. That's his sales distinction. He has the image of a tuxedo on his business card and "Tux" is his sales nickname. Customers have a hard time forgetting Tux. How could they? He is consistently among the top group of salespeople in the country for his particular automobile manufacturer.

Having been in sales for more than 20 years, I've learned a few effective tactics to progressively distinguish myself from the common salesman. While limos, tuxedos, and theater trips are great, you don't need to make such grand gestures in terms of time, money, and effort to differentiate yourself. There are plenty of little things you can do every day that will set you apart from other salespeople in your industry. These distinctions have worked for me, and they will work for you.

Twelve Leaps to Distinction

1. **Follow up immediately.** Don't wait, and don't procrastinate. I add a new prospect to my database the very same day I meet him or her. At this moment, I've put a complete follow up infrastructure in motion. Regardless of the economy, changes in technology, additions to my staff, the balance in my bank account, or whether I'm away from the office, my follow-up system is on automatic pilot. It is a simple and efficient process in which I contact my prospects and clients from time to time by using a series of mailed material, e-mailed information, and consistent e-mail updates. This guarantees my ability to connect with everyone with whom I communicate, without exceptions. It is set for life until they opt out.

2. **Deliver added value by doing something extra** for your customer or client *after* you've made the sale. I plan to spend some additional time, at no charge, when I consult with a company. Usually, I'll meet with salespeople for some one-on-one coaching. If the client is local, I make certain to accompany them on one of their face-to-face sales presentations during my six-month coaching program, or I sit in on one of their sales phone calls. If they're not local, then I can observe and listen to a sales call over a conference telephone call or during a webinar. Whatever the sales circumstance may be, I don't charge for my time.

3. **Network clients.** Many of my clients across the country know one another, something that is possible because I put them in touch with one another. I recently coordinated an exchange program between two of my largest clients—one based in Florida, the other in Texas. The two clients are in similar

industries but are not competitors. A sales manager from the Texas company flew with me to Florida to spend a day with that client; the vice president from Florida spent a day in Dallas with the vice president of the Texas company. The new environment that each executive encountered introduced them to new perspectives on day-to-day operations and tactics. This has improved productivity and enhanced the corporate culture for both companies.

If you have a client whom you think might benefit professionally from meeting another one of your clients, then by all means, introduce them. They will not only learn from one another, they'll be grateful to you for giving them the opportunity to see how other companies work, and for significantly expanding their networks.

4. **Have a manicure.** May 18, 1996, will always live in my memory as the day I learned that manicures are not for women only—and the day I paid $1,000 to be trained by Nido Qubein.

Nido is president of High Point University in High Point, North Carolina, chairman of Great Harvest Bread Company, an entrepreneur with interests in banking, advertising, and real estate, and former president of the National Speakers Association. Nido has traveled the world as a speaker and consultant addressing business and professional groups. These are the accomplishments of a man who immigrated to this country as a teenager from Lebanon without knowing a word of English. However, on that day in May, Nido spoke about concepts that were so strange to me, it was almost as though he were speaking a foreign language.

"Chuck, are you serious about your business?" Nido asked.

"Yes, of course," I replied.

"Then I want you to have your nails manicured."

After a few moments of shocked silence, I said, "Nido, I live in Texas. I fish for bass. I'm not so sure about that idea. It makes me feel very uncomfortable."

He simply responded, "Chuck, if you're serious about your business, then you'll have your nails manicured."

Eventually, I took Nido's advice and had a manicure—and I've been having them ever since. I know it sounds strange at first, but the truth is that someone with clean, manicured nails is distinctive. It shows that you make an effort with your appearance, and will be likely to make an effort in most other areas as well. If your customers see that you take care of yourself, *then they will feel confident that you'll take care of them as well.*

5. **Upgrade your wardrobe.** Whether you sit in a cubicle making phone calls and never lay eyes on a client, or see clients only once in a while, or spend every single day with clients, you need to **dress for success.** I can't tell you how many times I have gone into an office and seen salespeople who are dressed as if they were about to change the oil in their car or go dancing at a nightclub. Purchasing well-made, quality business clothing is making an investment in yourself. Have a suit or dress tailor-made; there are affordable options for tailored clothing. Make sure you are fitted properly with good material. Polish your shoes. Women and men can choose handsome purses or attaché cases. If you want to attain a high level of income in the future, then you need the right kind of clothing *now.* Enhancing your wardrobe speaks volumes to clients and boosts your self-esteem and confidence.

6. **Stop relying on text-only e-mails.** The next generation of e-mail communication has already arrived. Instead of typing a message, **send a video or audio message**. This is an easy and inexpensive way to distinguish yourself from the competition.

7. **Be a calligrapher.** Buy a calligraphy pen and use it when writing thank you notes or other handwritten correspondence to your top clients. A message written in a way that requires skill and care lets clients know they are important to you. Clients are much more likely to save and even display a beautifully handwritten note than a hurried e-mail—it will constantly remind them of you and your services.

8. **Get yourself some coaching.** Steve Langham, a businessman, entrepreneur, and millionaire who has had an extremely positive effect on my life, once said, "Highly successful people reach out for counseling, coaching, and training when they don't need it. The rest of the world reaches out when they do need it." *To improve professionally or personally, reach out to people who can help you.* Don't be the Lone Ranger. Instead, tap into support systems. I work with several coaches to maintain and improve my physical health, my financial security, and my spiritual well-being. They make me a better person, and I am happy to pay them for their knowledge and effect.

9. **Stay fit and healthy.** Your physical health and fitness greatly affect your professional performance. The two are inherently intertwined; your body is with you 24 hours a day, both on the job and off. Do what's necessary to be healthy. You have to eat every day, so choose foods that are energizing. Although it's quick and easy to grab food on the run, fast food will actually *slow* you down, so make smarter decisions during mealtime. Exercise to stay fit or to lose weight, if necessary. It doesn't necessarily come easily; you must work at improving and preserving good health. But the payoff, both personally and professionally, makes the effort entirely worthwhile. It will save you time and money for the rest of your life.

10. **Listen.** Listening requires very little effort and yet, for something that seems so easy, it is the weak link in the skill set of many salespeople. And, of course, the typical salesperson will disregard the thought of training in this area. So *don't be typical*. You can start listening to your clients right now. All you have to do is **stop talking**. Furthermore, don't interrupt when clients are speaking, and don't talk over their words. I've coached thousands of sales calls, and I can assure you that most salespeople talk until they're blue. When I listen in on sales phone calls, I sometimes hear a few sudden gasps from the client as if she is trying to say something but can't get a word in. I tell the salesperson, "Quick! Call 911! Your client is choking! . . .

because you won't let her speak!" Many salespeople don't even notice when a client is trying to talk.

Don't be that kind of salesperson. Don't be so wrapped up in your sales pitch that you can't even stop to hear what your clients have to say. Clients don't want to hear a lecture *from* you; they want to have a conversation *with* you. Clients remember a salesperson who listens. Listening is a sales superpower.

11. **Send noticeable mail.** This is what I like to call "crazy" mail, when you send something that ensures that the recipient opens the envelope. People tend to ignore mail that arrives in a formal white envelope. So step number one is **use colored envelopes.** I have nearly 8,000 colored envelopes in my office. I've even surveyed my clients around the country to determine which color receives the highest response—and the answer is pink. That's right: pink is the best marketing color, because it gets noticed. Strange, you say? Maybe so, but it's been proven that pink sells.

12. **Establish a sales process.** Instituting a sales process guarantees that you won't need to spend time thinking about what comes next. Your sales process will run as smoothly as Henry Ford's Model T assembly line. Regardless of how information arrives—by phone, by personal referral, or by e-mail—*a fixed process will enhance your ability to create revenue* from that information.

These 12 steps are a great start; however, they're just a few of the ideas you can use to accomplish sales stardom. Some might need to be modified to fit your specific sales processes and cycles, and there are certainly others that would be especially distinctive within your industry. Consider which distinctions—both personal and professional—you can incorporate into your sales process. Once you begin, two distinctive bunnies become twenty and, before you know it, you have your own bunny farm of distinctions. And you will have created a new brand called *you*!

Success Traits

Sales distinctions are individualized practices: one man hires a limousine to drive customers to and from his office, while another wears a tuxedo. Success traits, on the other hand, are universal. Regardless of the type of industry or the length of sales cycle, and no matter whether you are a beginner or a veteran, or are selling a household product or a financial service, there are five key traits that all highly successful salespeople have in common: **discipline, tenacity, implementation, focus,** and **desire.**

Every salesperson possesses a low, medium, or high level of each of these key ingredients to success. Some may have a low level of one or more traits, others will have medium levels of some or all the traits, and still others will be so fortunate as to have high levels of all traits. The formula for the greatest success is obvious: maintaining high levels of all five traits while running on all cylinders provides the "horsepower" that it takes to reach the top of the sales ladder.

Discipline

Substantial attention to **discipline** is a must for those who want to succeed in sales. Discipline means forming the **daily habits** that are necessary to produce more revenue for you and your company. Discipline and habits go hand-in-hand. Become disciplined and habits will be formed over time. Many self-help and personal development books state that habits can be established in 21 days; however, I need to raise the bulls—t flag on that. How many "21-day habits" have you truly developed and stuck with for more than 2.1 hours? Then was it really a habit? Probably not. Habits take *much* longer to form. I have learned from coaching hundreds of people over the years that a habit requires closer to 210 days of continual practice to become firmly entrenched.

The level beyond habit is *unconscious competency*. You become unconsciously competent at a given task once you've performed a habit for so long that you no longer think about the action—you simply do it. When you are unconsciously competent in all of your sales methods, that's when you will stop overthinking the think, and instead overdo the do.

Tenacity

Another key ingredient for sales success is **tenacity**. *A salesperson must exhibit an all-or-nothing attitude when performing revenue-producing activities.* The next chapter of this book is not entitled "Marketing Yourself Timidly." You cannot market yourself timidly and expect to succeed. *Timid salespeople have skinny kids.* Remember that. You must achieve a high level of tenacity and, once you do, there is no limit to what you can accomplish. This comes through in a salesperson's walk, talk, focus, and white-hot burning desire to give everything a 100 percent effort at *all times*. Salespeople with tenacity are *completely* engaged; there's no middle ground with them, and they never leave anything to chance.

Implementation

Rounding out the top three success traits is **implementation**. Surprisingly, many salespeople manage to talk themselves *out* of implementing good habits that will create revenue. For example, when I lead a workshop for salespeople in the financial industry, someone in the audience always says, "I can't do that because of my compliance department." This rebuttal is not only an unwillingness to implement, but it's also a display of the wrong kind of attitude. The fact is that most compliance departments are usually receptive to new ideas that are properly and professionally presented. *Your sales will increase if you find reasons to implement rather than reasons not to implement.* (See Figure 1.1.)

Focus

You must **focus** and concentrate on work. Don't allow distractions to impede your success. One common distraction happens every day

discipline
tenacity
implementation

WORK SMART
MAKE MORE
IN LESS TIME!

chuckbauer.com ~ cbsalestools.com

FIGURE 1.1

around the world at 11:15 A.M. What do salespeople, sales managers, and sales organizations do at that time? They start thinking about lunch. If there were such a thing as a focus measurement meter, it would register a sharp decline among salespeople between 11:14 A.M. and 11:15 A.M. Don't take the focus off your revenue-producing activities by spending time pondering who to have lunch with and where to eat.

Another time-wasting activity is talking or texting on a cell phone. If the communication is not sales-related, then it's a distraction—period. Use your time wisely. An illustration of this is a coaching experience I had with a saleswoman. I was present during some of her sales calls, and when the calls were finished I left her office, slowly counted to 10, and then walked back in to find her texting on her cell phone.

Salespeople think they work eight-hour days, but the time devoted to sales is realistically closer to three or four hours. *Be aware of activities and thoughts that steal your focus.*

Desire

The last of the five universal success traits is **desire**. In 1999, I consulted for an advertising/business evaluation company for which the top salesman was a man named Gene. He was college-educated, very professional, extremely tenacious, a sharp dresser, and rarely failed to close a deal.

Then there was mild and meek Fred. He did not have a college degree, he dressed in jeans, a sloppy shirt, and cowboy boots, and before joining the company he drove 18-wheelers cross-country. Yet over time, Fred worked his way up to the number-two spot in sales; he even challenged Gene for the top spot in some months. What did Fred have that made up for all the things he didn't have? A white-hot burning *desire* to succeed. He was willing to do anything, learn whatever was necessary, work as hard as he could, be as smart as possible, do his best, and maximize his time in order to reach the top sales position in the company and provide for his family.

■ ■ ■

Discipline, tenacity, implementation, focus, and desire—these five success traits are the most important among the hundreds of factors that will take you to the top of your sales organization. You want to strive to achieve the highest levels of these qualities at all times. Can you do it overnight? No. Can you reach such a goal in a year? Yes, you most certainly can.

As you incorporate both the distinctions and traits mentioned above into your sales process during the year, remember these three little words: *extraordinary, average,* and *mediocre.* (See Figure 1.2.)

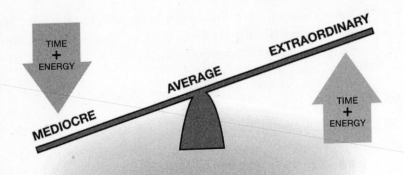

Your **ACTIVITY** and **ATTITUDE** make the difference!

www.chuckbauer.com   •   www.cbsalestools.com

FIGURE 1.2

If you are now an average salesperson, then the amount of time and energy required to move up to "extraordinary" is the same as the amount that is needed to sink to "mediocre." Only your attitude and the activities in which you engage will make the difference. For instance, in every office there is the salesperson who arrives at 8:00 A.M. and heads straight for the coffeepot. Down the hall is the salesperson who came in at 7:45 A.M. and began working.

Speaking of coffee, let's return to our discussion of lunchtime behavior. There are plenty of salespeople who, at around 11:15 A.M., start thinking about which buddies to have lunch with and what they feel like eating. There are other salespeople, however, who— realizing that they don't have a prospective client to take to lunch— decide to close the office door, lock it, eat lunch at their desks, and not let anyone or anything interfere with their revenue-producing activity.

The time and energy required are the same in both examples; only the attitudes and activities are different. If you commit to activities that advance your sales process, then you will rise to "extraordinary" rather than sink to "mediocre."

Quick Tips to Achieve Distinction

Follow up immediately.

Do something extra for clients at no additional charge.

Introduce your clients to one another and/or get involved with Sales Coach Chuck's exchange program.

Men, get a manicure.

Invest in professional attire.

Begin using the next generation of e-mail today—send video or audio messages.

Write notes with a calligraphy pen to your top clients.

Reach out to people who can help you personally and professionally.

Stay fit and healthy.

Stop talking and start listening.

Send mail that will be opened.

Establish a sales process and follow it.

Three Groups of Salespeople: 3-Percenters, 27-Percenters, and 70-Percenters

Related to the notion of the three groups of extraordinary, average, and mediocre salespeople, the clothing tag of the sales world lists its raw materials as 3 percent top sales producers, 27 percent average performers, and 70 percent minimal inputters. (See Figure 1.3.) We'll begin by examining the 70-percenters, because that's the category in which the majority of salespeople are and will remain.

These salespeople repeatedly jump from one company to another. They don't work on improving their sales skills; instead, they work only hard enough to stay one sale away from losing their job. Actually, 70-percenters are almost always on the fence between quitting and getting fired. As a result, I encourage sales managers to never allow 70-percenters to pierce the corporate veil. Initially, sales managers should conduct a phone interview with a candidate;

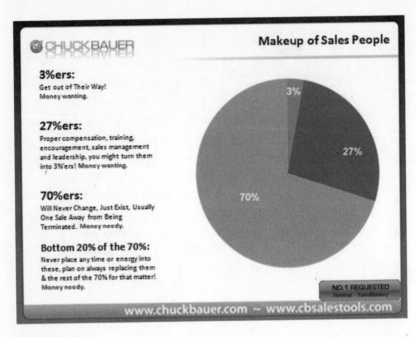

FIGURE 1.3

if they find that he's a 70-percenter, then do not offer him a sales job. If one is hired somehow, escort him out the door.

The adage years ago was that the bottom rung made up 80 percent of a company's sales force, and the other 20 percent were the top performers. That is no longer true. I have observed salespeople in a variety of industries around the world and most of them—70 percent of them—are in this bottom category. The company they work for or the structure of the sales organization makes no difference; 70-percenters are at the mercy of their own attitudes and behaviors.

If you are a 70-percenter, then know this: you have the capacity to rise when you break through your preconceived notions about selling and are willing to change, when you become fully engaged in your sales career and don't simply mark time, and when you want money more than you need money. There's a big difference between wanting money and needing money. This group *needs* money simply to pay bills. The smaller groups, the 3-percenters and 27-percenters, *want* money for security and indulgences.

With the proper motivation, encouragement, structure, support, sales tools, and out-of-the-box training, a 27-percenter may aspire to become a 3-percenter, but will be content to achieve the earnings of a 27-percenter. That's fine; they fill the category that brings in most of the revenue. Twenty-seven percenters are a sales organization's safety net, the bread and butter. These are the salespeople who stay with a company for a long time. They want money for life's little pleasures, such as vacations and big-screen TVs.

Finally, there are the 3-percenters, who will from now on be referred to as F.O.N.s, or *Freaks of Nature*. If you are in a hiring position and have a little luck, then you might manage to get a F.O.N. on board. And once the F.O.N. is on board, get out of the way. F.O.N.s do not need any help. They require nothing from you except a great commission structure. Like the 27-percenters, they too want money—but not for purchasing power. They want money for their families, their savings, and their personal insurance. F.O.N.s build impenetrable walls of security around themselves with the money they earn in sales. They are hungry. They are hunters. They are competitive. F.O.N.s have personalities similar to one another; they are usually dominant, somewhat social, extremely driven, and very independent. Of course, they always maintain high levels of discipline, tenacity, implementation, focus, and desire. They are extraordinary in everything they do, and therefore they earn the distinction of being in the top 3 percent of salespeople.

I have had the good fortune to work with some of these salespeople in several companies. But no matter the company or the product, F.O.N.s all possess certain characteristics and skills. Some of these come naturally, but some are learned—which means that you too can adopt the following characteristics and skills.

F.O.N.s are *extremely* serious about their business. They are professional closers, or PCs, rather than professional visitors, or PVs. PVs are typically better suited to customer service roles rather than sales positions. They are professional information providers, but they don't close sales and they don't increase revenue.

PCs, on the other hand, are closing sales *all the time*. There is no situation in which they are afraid to ask for the order. If the client remarks, "You know what? I don't like you," then the salesperson will respond, "Well, despite that, are you ready to proceed with the order?" If the customer says, "I don't like anyone in Texas," then the professional closer comes back with, "Now that we have that out of the way, and based on what I've shown you, are you ready to complete the paperwork and pay for the order?"

F.O.N.s major in major-league activities. They don't get involved in office politics or drama, and they choose their sales buddies carefully. You will never, ever hear a F.O.N. gossiping with their colleagues. They simply do not engage in minor-league office antics. As professional closers, F.O.N.s are focused on their daily goals, on the calls they must make, and on the face-to-face appointments they must keep. They are not projects.

F.O.N.s maintain an ownership mentality. Whether they actually own the company or are a salesperson, sales manager, or sales executive of someone else's company, F.O.N.s always act as if the company belongs to them. This attitude supports their tendency to take their sales seriously. When the company provides sales leads, these salespeople go after them as if they had spent their own money on the leads. Moreover, they fully own every situation—routine or challenging, success or failure. They never lapse into thinking that they are "just an employee."

A salesperson with the "employee mentality" waits for the company to provide what she needs to make a sale. In one of my workshops, I explain the importance of standing during a phone call in order to release the diaphragm for a more commanding voice. A woman in the audience once raised her hand and said, "I can't stand up in my office."

"Why can't you stand?" I asked.

"Because the cord to my headset isn't long enough."

Rather than spend $5.00 to buy a longer cord, she was actually waiting for the company to give her one. That's "employee" mentality.

F.O.N.s are extraordinary communicators. In sales, a good communicator is someone who knows how to reach masses of people with the touch of a button using automated systems. And they listen to their clients—*really* listen. They make sure their products and services are solving a clients' specific problem or meeting an underlying need, no matter what.

F.O.N.s are also extraordinary presenters, whether over the phone, face-to-face, or via a web format. Clients believe what a F.O.N. says about his company, the product he is selling, and himself. F.O.N.s don't achieve this simply by pitching; they pitch, yes, but they also *tell stories* that give their clients strong visual images. They provide client testimonials or examples that elevate the client's ability to truly believe what they're saying. Once the salesperson is able to instill this kind of confidence in the client, the client no longer has any fear, uncertainty, or doubt (otherwise known as F.U.D.).

F.O.N.s are also coachable, consistent, and work *smart* versus working *hard*. When I coach a F.O.N. on a sales call, they never become defensive or try to rationalize what they've said. I offer a suggestion for improvement and she simply says, "Okay, I'll change that on the next call." F.O.N.s are flexible and open to changes; they know that this approach is necessary to navigate the turbulent waters of sales processes.

Consistency is important—and F.O.N.s know this. Repeating the proper activities on a daily basis drives revenue. One of my coaching students recently spent two hours in my office on one of my ordinary sales days. As she left she remarked, "You know what I saw today? That you do the right things over and over and over again." Consistency works.

F.O.N.s choose to work smart. Consider this analogy: you're walking along the street and suddenly a voice in your head instructs you to look down.

There in front of you on the sidewalk is a $100 bill and a $10 bill. The voice says that you can only take one—not both. Which bill would you pick up? The $100 or the $10? (See Figure 1.4.) The $100 bill, of course. In practice, however, most salespeople do not pick up the $100. They pick up $10 even though $100 is staring them right in the face.

Consider your health and fitness, both of which greatly influence your sales performance. When you go to lunch, do you choose foods that provide energy or foods that slow you down? Are you

www.chuckbauer.com • www.cbsalestools.com

FIGURE 1.4

having lunch with colleagues or prospects? When the day ends, some salespeople race to the bar to engage in both personally and professionally destructive behavior. Are they choosing the $100 bill or the $10 bill? Others go home, get the family settled down after dinner, and then watch a 10-minute YouTube video on how to increase sales. This costs nothing, but the potential gains are enormous. Have they grabbed $100 or $10?

Sometimes, however, choosing the $100 bill does have a price. For instance, spending a day in training with Nido Qubein cost me $1,000 in 1996. But that investment proved to be more than worthwhile, because I have been able to convert what I learned in one day into millions of dollars in sales. Thus it's really quite simple. Your thoughts and actions dictate which bill you choose. So approach the sidewalk like a F.O.N. and grab the $100.

Another important characteristic of F.O.N.s is that they are passionate and enthusiastic about their company, their product, and themselves. They keep one important thing in mind: *ignorance on fire always out-sells knowledge on ice.*

What exactly does that mean? A recent survey taken by a business magazine asked clients who recently purchased financial products what mattered most to them about their salesperson. "Enthusiasm" was cited as the most important quality, while "product knowledge" actually mattered *least*. Many salespeople tend to highlight their factual knowledge of a product and de-emphasize their enthusiasm. F.O.N.s are enthused by what they do and what they sell. I worked with one typically mild-mannered client who, on one particular day, was all fired up, talking and acting like a F.O.N. Why? Because he needed to make $500 to buy his wife a new set of tires. Though I couldn't help but wonder whether or not his enthusiasm continued the next day, at that moment he was driven by a goal and was not going to be deterred.

Finally, F.O.N.s have a solid work ethic. They start the workday early and maximize their time. Lunch is not a distraction: there's no playtime, and they do not slip into a country-club mentality. They never have their feet on the desk, and they don't hang out around the coffeepot chitchatting and eating donuts. Instead, they spend their time on activities that make money for them and for their company. They pick up that $100 bill at every opportunity.

You too can be a F.O.N. if you choose the thought patterns and daily activities that maximize your day. See the box titled "Become a Freak of Nature in the Sales World" for a list of the habits, tactics, and attitudes of a F.O.N.

Become a Freak of Nature in the Sales World

- Be a professional closer (PC) rather than a professional visitor (PV).
- Stay away from office politics, drama, and gossip. Don't be a project. Sell as if you own the company.
- Communicate with *and listen to* your clients.
- Master the art of presenting.

(continued)

(*Continued*)

- Accept coaching; don't argue with the coach and make excuses for your habits.
- Perform revenue-producing activities with consistency.
- Work smart: always pick up the $100 bill rather than the $10.
- Exude enthusiasm about your company, your product, and yourself.
- Embrace a strong work ethic.

Sales Distinctions and Success Traits Commission Development Quiz

Anything fewer than 100 percent correct answers requires immediate additional work!

1. The five main sales traits that will help you get to the top of the sales ladder are:

   D_____

   T_____

   I_____

   F_____

   D_____

2. Which one of the above traits is described as forming the habit on a daily basis that produces revenue?

(*Continued*)

3. Complete this mantra: "Don't overthink the think;

   _____."

   Remember, it takes 210 days of developing a habit to get to the point of becoming the *unconscious competent*!

4. Regarding tenacity, Sales Coach Chuck points out that "Timid salespeople have _____!"

5. On implementation, Sales Coach Chuck says, "Find the reasons to do it, instead of finding _____ _____."

6. Even with varying levels of the other success traits, having the highest levels of this trait can provide some leverage against having lower levels of the others. What trait is this?

7. "If everyone else is doing it, S-T-O-_!"

8. What are four methods of achieving distinction?
   A._____ (Relates to follow-up)

   B._____ (This is one you can implement today—right now)

   C._____ (What you're not going to see in a post office)

   D._____ (Keeps you from having to think to produce revenue)

(*continued*)

(Continued)

9. True or false: Your professional and personal lives are intertwined.

    Reflect: What distinctions are you going to work on professionally?

    What distinctions are you going to work on personally?

10. If you're average, the energy and time it takes to get to extraordinary is the same effort required to transition from average to mediocre. It's your _____ and your _____ that make the difference.

11. Name two attitudes or behaviors of a F.O.N. (Freak of Nature) in pursuing sales.

12. Name two reasons that people are unsuccessful in sales or remain at the lower 70 percent performance level.

13. Why are you not completing this quiz?

Sales Distinctions and Success Traits Quiz Answers

1. Discipline, tenacity, implementation, focus, and desire

2. Discipline

3. Overdo the do

(continued)

(*Continued*)

4. Skinny kids

5. The reasons not to do it

6. Desire

7. P

8. A. Immediacy

   B. Listening

   C. Pink (or colored) envelopes

   D. Having a set sales process

9. True

10. Attitude/activities

11. Any two of these: they're professional closers, major in major league activities, have an ownership mentality, are extraordinary communicators, are extraordinary presenters, are coachable, consistent, and work smart versus working hard, and they have a strong work ethic.

12. Lazy, only want money to pay bills, Lone Rangers, "employee mentality"

13. Any excuse will do, right?

2

Marketing Yourself Shamelessly

As soon as a prospect walks through your door, the sales process begins. Whether you realize it or not, they will immediately begin judging you on hundreds of things every few seconds—from your handshake or greeting to the way you dress, to the way you talk, and on and on. However, there are three critical judgments that surpass the influence of any others—and that have everything to do with getting and closing the sale. (See Figure 2.1.) These three are the client's impressions of:

1. You as a salesperson.
2. Your company.
3. Your product.

Notice that this chapter is not titled Marketing Your *Company* Shamelessly or Marketing Your *Product* Shamelessly. You are

and then offer their reasonings and excuses as to why. However, there's really a simple reason for this: if their score is less than 20, they are experiencing F.U.D.! You are not going to close any business when F.U.D. exists. If you can develop your sales skills to the highest level and can consistently score at least 20—and work your way up to 30—then you will have moved closer to closing the deal.

Think of each category as a gas tank. You have to figure out how to get your sales levels up and keep them as high as possible at all times. Using this scorecard and practicing the Sales Mastery principles is the most effective psychological tool—*if* you score yourself candidly. Even when your tanks have fallen below the necessary accomplishment levels, you can get back on track by using the tactics taught in this book to move your score back up, and thereby consistently secure more sales.

If you *are* consistently closing sales, chances are that you are at 20 points or above on the scorecard, but you aren't liable to find yourself at a peak score of 30 until you begin to work on your sales habits and techniques. Practice the methods introduced in this chapter and then rate yourself again. Your psychogenic score is apt to increase, as will your sales numbers. Continue to market yourself shamelessly and you will gain your client's confidence and their willingness to recommend you to other customers; accomplish this, and I'll nominate you for a Nobel Peace Prize for finding the cure for F.U.D.

The process of marketing yourself shamelessly will help you build a referral-based business. You won't be dumping dollars on marketing techniques that don't deliver a satisfactory return, such as unnecessary advertisements, services that offer leads, and telemarketing firms. Instead, your client base will deliver new clients to you.

Another benefit of marketing yourself shamelessly is that you will **become bulletproof** to typical sales challenges, such as prospects and clients who don't answer your phone calls, return your voicemail messages, reply to your e-mails, or bother to keep appointments with you—and also those who just plain don't like you. Market yourself shamelessly and you will make more for yourself and your company.

Keep Everyone Talking . . . about *You*

Silence is the one thing that's sure to vanquish your sales super-power among your clients and prospects. An important aspect of actively selling yourself is making certain your sales contacts are talking about you. You want them automatically to think of you first when they are ready to enter the marketplace. Establishing a Top of Mind Awareness campaign—or a T.O.M.A. campaign, as I'll refer to it—lets you directly influence what your prospects and clients are saying about you by communicating with them regularly. While most salespeople communicate consistently before they make the sale, the level of communication drops significantly afterward. *A T.O.M.A. campaign establishes an ongoing system of communication for before* and *after the sale*. T.O.M.A. also generates referrals by get-ting salespeople into the habit of *asking for them*. Admittedly, most people in sales are too lazy to ask. (Who's ever heard of a lazy sales superhero? Oxymoronic, isn't it?) T.O.M.A. campaigns encourage salespeople to implement a system-based referral response program as a regular part of their company's policy and procedure. A typical program will include one-to-seven activities, such as asking for a referral before concluding a phone call, or at the end of an e-mail or letter. Another tactic might require scheduling a block of time to call existing clients for referrals, or creating an e-mail newsletter that specifically asks for them.

Having an established sales referral program is vital to your sales success. How many referral techniques are you currently using? I'm guessing that your answer might rhyme with hero. If you're not getting referrals, you're not asking the right way. Did you even earn the right to ask? Would *you* buy from you?

A T.O.M.A. campaign will also help you avoid sales jeopardy—that time period of purgatory when your prospect has not yet given you a yes or no answer. Most salespeople don't do anything when they're in sales jeopardy, regardless of how much time passes. A power-packed T.O.M.A. campaign, however, pro-vides an autonomic and steady flow of continuous communication with that person. As a result, when your prospects are ready to buy, they will not turn to Google or your competitor as a source. They will remember *you*—because you created T.O.M.A.

Here's a perfect example of how a T.O.M.A. campaign can rescue an otherwise lost business deal. Dallas Cooley is a client of mine in Gainesville, Georgia. He is president of Georgia Powder Coating Company. Dallas had been trying to close a deal with the city of Marietta, Georgia, for some time when suddenly all communication stopped. Dallas called me and said, "We've got them in the T.O.M.A. campaign, but they're not responding to anything. So I'm moving on to other opportunities." And that's what he did.

A few weeks later, Dallas called me again. He had received an e-mail from the city manager of Marietta confirming a purchase order worth $70,000. The order was a result of the automated communication system Dallas had *set up at the start* of his relationship with the city. Despite the break in communication, the deal successfully closed—because Dallas used a Marketing Yourself Shamelessly tactic.

A T.O.M.A. campaign consists of **five stages that build one upon the other**. These five stages are all strengthened by the Six Rules of Effective T.O.M.A., which are:

1. **You must be courageous.** Don't allow your ego to persuade you not to engage in activities that involve out-of-the-box thinking.

2. Don't overthink the think; **overdo the do**.

3. Only **after six to eight touches** will you begin to penetrate your client or prospect's consciousness to cause a sales or referral reaction.

4. **Do the work once, and then forget about it.** Use the power of discipline, tenacity, and action to establish a program for contacting all of your clients and prospects regularly. After doing all the work one time.

5. *Stop* **using the same marketing methods** as everyone else. Instead, find a better, more distinctive way to market yourself.

www.chuckbauer.com • www.cbsalestools.com

FIGURE 2.3

6. **Don't be lazy or complacent**. (See Figure 2.3.) Though the lazy approach may seem easier, you'll pay the price when you're forced to watch your competitors make the money you're not making due to your laziness.

Some of these rules should look familiar from Chapter 1: Sales Distinctions and Success Traits. T.O.M.A. is all about being distinctive. Much of the sales world walks the same path. For example, when I ask people to hold up their business cards during a seminar, I see a bunch of cards that all look the same. Each is only another grain of sand in the desert of nondistinction. Distinctive marketing and sales tools as mapped out in a T.O.M.A. campaign builds layer upon layer of awareness in your client's mind.

The Five Stages of T.O.M.A.

Now that the rules are set, let's implement the Five Stages of T.O.M.A, the first of which deals with Microsoft Outlook. Since the great majority of personal computer users have Outlook, you should, too. **Every person you know**—a client, a prospect, a friend, a relative, an acquaintance, absolutely everyone—**should be logged into your Outlook.** You must input and keep track of your contacts with discipline. This will make the practice become a habit, and you eventually become unconsciously competent in this procedure.

Don't just stop at inputting basic information, either; along with each person's name, mailing address, phone number, and e-mail address, include their birthdays and hobbies or passions as well. You can manipulate this information to your advantage later. But how do you find out things like new prospects' birthdays and hobbies? Simple—ask about them!

When I meet a prospect face-to-face, I look them in the eye; when we talk on the phone, I have command in my voice. I usually say something to the effect of "Thank you for sharing that valuable information with me in regards to your specific needs and challenges. I actually have something of significance to share with you. I consider all of my client interactions to be *lifelong relationships*. Every person, every prospect, and every client with whom I come in contact is treated that way. Therefore, I do have two questions for you. First, what is the month and day of your birth? I ask that because I might be doing something special for you on your birthday. Second, if you were to take a week off on vacation, what would we find you doing? What passion or hobby would you be pursuing during your free time?"

By utilizing this information, you will be able to reach out to prospects in distinctive and memorable ways. For example, on any given day, I have five or more clients with birthdays. Rare is the day that does not list a single birthday. I do not send birthday cards; that's not really very distinctive. Instead, on that day, my contacts receive a video or audio e-mail in which I mention their name and where we met. And thanks to Outlook, my birthday wishes are never belated.

One of my clients works for Thomson Reuters in Dexter, Michigan. I've sent him a birthday video for four consecutive years. After receiving the most recent one, he called and said, "I never get tired of your personalized birthday videos." That's someone who I can count on for at least one significant referral per year. In fact, I can consider all of my birthday videos as referrals that are waiting to happen. Another client showed his video to people in his office. That afternoon, one of his colleagues left me a message, saying that he was ready to talk about coaching. These videos are one of the many reasons I don't need to spend money on advertising.

I was once told, "Chuck, I know how to use Outlook, but you know how to maximize Outlook." Outlook is the greatest client management tool known to man . . . *if it's maximized properly.* Many of Outlook's features will create revenue or buy back valuable time through automation, organization, and tracking. To learn more, I highly recommend reading Jim Boyce's *Microsoft Outlook 2010 Plain & Simple* or *Microsoft Outlook 2007 Plain & Simple.*

The second stage of your T.O.M.A. campaign pertains to follow-up, one of the 12 Steps to Distinction explained in Chapter 1. Every new contact should *immediately* receive the *Excerpts from the Treasury of Quotes* by Jim Rohn, a small book (3.5 by 5 inches, to be exact) which elicits *big* results. The reason for giving your contacts this little-yet-powerful book is simple: hundreds of my students have sent it to clients over the years and it's always proved to have a positive effect. Though we have beta-tested other gifts and books over time, none has managed to match the positive results garnered from sending this particular gift to clients. Use this book as your top-secret weapon to create a positive first impression.

Sharing this book with clients puts you ahead of your competition for three reasons:

1. You **distinguish yourself** by doing something that the rest of the sales pack does not. Through a seemingly simple gesture, you immediately create a positive first impression. And, of course, you never get a second chance to create that positive first impression.

2. You will **secure respect** by sending this book because you are doing something out of the ordinary for a prospect. One of the many reasons why prospects don't return phone calls, don't respond to e-mails, or don't fulfill their appointments

is simply that they don't respect you. They expect that you will be just like all the other salespeople they've encountered. Giving your contact this book helps you earn respect because you are showing that you are indeed different from the others. It helps you overcome those lack-of-respect challenges while you initiate the first point of contact.

3. As the law of reciprocity implies, most prospects **will want to do something in return** for you. Here's the perfect testament to the power of this phenomenon. On a business trip to Houston, Texas, I spent a day in observation at a furniture store owned by Mac McInvale that is already benefiting from a tit-for-tat sales scenario. First of all, the store has its own restaurant right next to their space. So when a customer is on the fence in deciding whether to purchase, the salesperson graciously and generously suggests that they go into the restaurant to enjoy a bite on his tab while mulling over the decision. He walks the potential customer into the restaurant and instructs the waitstaff to put the meal on his tab. The customer is so completely wowed by this generosity that they frequently decide to buy—because they feel they "owe" the salesperson. This is the perfect example of how this type of sales psychology can make your job easier.

Be aware of the fact that while many prospects won't necessarily respond without delay, they do typically reply after receiving *Excerpts from the Treasury of Quotes*. Caution: don't mail the Jim Rohn books to a few people and then give up if they don't respond favorably. That's just lazy. **Remember: only mass action will bring you mass results.** If you wanted to catch as many fish as possible in the ocean, would you cast just a few hooks—or would you throw out as many nets as possible? Once your seeds are sown in a garden, do you focus more on the seeds that didn't sprout—or are you looking at the new corn crop that grew from the kernels that did take root? Send the books to prospects, current clients, *and* former clients. Done with discipline over time, the return on mass action is an increase in revenue from people who want to work with you.

Deciding whether to send *Excerpts from the Treasury of Quotes* to clients shouldn't require intense consideration, since the book's quotes are quite neutral. Any salesperson in any industry can confidently send the book and enjoy the associated benefits that come from having their clients receive it and read it. There is a dedication page at the front of the book on which you can write a personal note to your prospect or client. Insert your business card between the front cover and the dedication page, and then mail the book in a colored envelope that will capture the recipient's attention.

For the best results, use a **pink envelope** (as discussed in the last chapter) and do not include a return address; this will pique your contacts' curiosity and entice them to open the mail. White business envelopes are indistinguishable from one another, like simply another cloud in the sky. But a rainbow amid all the clouds is never unnoticed. Like you, your mail must be unique.

One of the audience members of my live Marketing Yourself Shamelessly course announced that if he received a pink envelope in the mail without a return address, he would throw it into the trash. That's fine, I told him, but be careful: don't let *your* attitude stand in the way of what will work for others 99 percent of the time. Even if you would throw away such an envelope, do you think the rest of the world necessarily would? Yes, some people might toss it out, but the majority will open the envelope. I've seen it happen with countless numbers of my own clients. Get out of your own way and put aside your preconceived notions about the color pink. This isn't about you; it's about how the majority of people will react to a pink envelope. A student and Sales Mastery graduate of mine sent the following e-mail to his sales staff: "You will all get a kick out of this. I just got a call back on one of the *pink envelopes* I sent out last week. They were totally impressed by the follow-up method, and it got the decision-maker's attention." Although some of these tactics might seem odd to you, I have witnessed many situations in which they *really worked* to get a potential client's attention.

Stage three of T.O.M.A. is sending unique and staggered mail pieces. The frequency of your mailings will depend on your sales cycle; the shorter the cycle, the shorter the mail campaign, while a longer sales cycle calls for more time between mailings. For example, I use the following staggered mail campaign designed for a one-month sales cycle. Once I've sent *Excerpts from the Treasury of Quotes* to a new contact, three other mailings go out to that person over the following three weeks. If the book is the first mailing, the second mailing is sent one week later, another piece of mail goes two weeks later, and a fourth item is mailed three weeks later. Each piece of mail builds on the previous and pitches a logical progression of information or storytelling. This allows me to communicate with a new contact four times over the course of one month.

Quick Items to Use for Reaching Out to Clients

1. *Excerpts from the Treasury of Quotes* by Jim Rohn.
2. A distinctive and nontemplate newsletter.
3. A Google image of the client's hobby or passion sent with a note that says "Saw this and thought of you."
4. A flyer with product information or how-to articles.
5. A one-page sales sheet that responds to the most common objections that you get from prospects.
6. A referral reminder.
7. A special offer.
8. A document with company information and industry articles.
9. A photo montage of buildings, offices, staff members, support teams, the company helping clients—any and all of these.
10. Information that might help a prospect navigate your website.
11. Previous and current client testimonials.
12. Product training tips.

Keeping this staggered mail system organized requires only an accordion folder with file compartments numbered 1 to 31 to indicate mailing dates. Each subsequent outreach should be prepared for mailing on the same day the book is sent. In other words, address, stuff, and stamp the envelopes on day one, then place them into the accordion folder according to the days they will be mailed. So if the initial package (which should be the book) happens to go out on the first of the month, then the second mailing is placed in the file for the seventh, the third for the fourteenth, and the fourth in the slot for the twenty-first. (If your sales cycle lasts two months, then you would send mail every two weeks to cover that time period.) This is an example of how you can *do the work once and then forget about it.*

As with the first stage of T.O.M.A.—when you're logging every new contact into Outlook—make this mailing procedure a discipline. It will, in turn, become a habit, which will then transform into yet another unconscious competency. The sooner you plant, the sooner you harvest.

The next stage of your T.O.M.A. campaign logically follows the staggered mail program—sending staggered *e-mails* to your contacts. These can be as simple as duplicating the mailed items, asking for a referral, pitching a certain product, or simply thanking someone for being a prospect. A strong e-mail campaign in tandem with your mail program will yield results.

Furthermore, these results grow exponentially as your client base expands. A student of mine named Jeff Dunn is with CRC Insurance in Atlanta, Georgia. When Jeff received a list of 190 additional contacts, he and his staff immediately sent each one a copy of Jim Rohn's book. They then prepared envelopes of marketing materials to go to each contact once a month for 12 months and e-mails to go out on an individual basis every other month. That is 2,900 mailings and 1,140 e-mails—a total of 3,420 touches to 190 people over a year—which was, except for trips to the mailbox, all *fully automated.* Jeff and his team did this in their spare time over the course of about a week to generate new sales, cross sales, and referrals. By achieving those kinds of numbers, they cannot miss.

Remember: you need to make six to eight touches to penetrate your client or prospect's awareness.

The fifth and final stage of T.O.M.A. requires that you utilize an e-mail marketing service provider such as iContact to issue a quarterly newsletter. iContact allows me to both disseminate a blanket e-mail newsletter to all of my clients, and gives me the added benefit of being able to track the number of times each person looks at the newsletter, and also to see exactly what he or she is reading. My sales staff then contacts the people who have the most clicks on the newsletter. Someone who looks at the newsletter 50 times would seemingly have more interest in sales training, sales coaching, or purchasing a sales tool than someone who's only viewed it once. A system such as iContact allows me and my sales team to follow up with the people who are most likely to do business with us.

More Ways to Create and Enhance a T.O.M.A. Campaign

When you're taking the time to send "snail mail" to clients, be sure to address each envelope by hand and do away with the return address. A hand-addressed envelope demands attention and an envelope without a return address is more likely to be opened by the recipient—that's the only way to find out who sent it. Keep in mind that without a return address, undeliverable mail won't be sent back to you. However, don't be concerned about contacts whose addresses have changed. The few that you lose track of won't matter, because you'll be occupying your time with clients who are doing business with you because of your T.O.M.A. campaign. *Don't look at the rearview mirror—look ahead through the front windshield and keep moving forward.*

In addition, a first-class postage stamp is a must—no metered mail. In his book *The Mercifully Brief Real World Guide to Raising $1,000 Gifts by Mail*, author Mal Warwick teaches charitable organizations how to raise money. He explains that above all else, mail must *look important.* To create this kind of eminent appearance, Warwick recommends ditching the "junk mail" look by avoiding the trappings of standard direct mail—such as bulk-rate postage, bar codes, inexpensive paper stock, and window envelopes with teasers printed on the front. Your time will be well-spent putting stamps on envelopes.

Apart from the staggered mail program that your T.O.M.A. campaign will regularly trigger, there are special letters that you can send to clients at the appropriate time. The first one is a play on the junk mail everyone receives, crumples, and throws away. At the top of your letter in large, bold, and colored print is the following message: "This letter is precrinkled so that it will be at home in your trash can. If you read the rest of the letter, however, you'll know whether or not you would benefit by meeting with me." The rest of the letter consists of your pitch. Then, crumple it, stomp on it and insert in a colored envelope. With such a mishandled letter inside, even the envelope will look a bit disheveled—which is sure to grab a prospective client's attention.

Another unique option is to send a letter to a client's pet. Begin with something such as, "Dear Elvis the Cat, Would you please let your owners know about . . . " and then continue with your pitch. Another idea is to write a letter to the product; for example, if you're a car salesman, send a letter to the car that the customer recently purchased. If you sold a blue Nissan ZX, address the envelope to that car, and then send something like the following:

Dear Nissan ZX,

It's time for your first oil change; 90 days have passed since you left the dealership. Please contact our service department or have your owners call to schedule your service.

By the way, I noticed that John and Sue—your owners—have not yet referred any business to me. The next time they start your ignition, please remind them that they owe their salesperson a referral.

One piece of mail to *not* send is a Christmas holiday card. Avoid this at all costs. The primary reason for this should be evident: everyone in the world does it. Therefore, sending a Christmas card will do nothing to set you apart from anyone else. Choose a different holiday to send cards, such as Valentine's Day or the Fourth of July. If you really feel that you must acknowledge the winter holidays in some way, treat your top 15 to 20 percent of clients to a night out or a special gift. *Remember: don't count the people you reach—reach the people who count.*

You might be wondering how much these kinds of efforts tend to cost. To give you an estimate of the budget for all of this correspondence, consider that my average monthly costs for mailing expenses—envelopes, printing, postage, and the book of quotes—are about $4.50 per person. However, whether I spend a total of $45 or $4,500, the results I reap from mail *far* outperform the results I'd receive spending the same amount on most advertising. Rather than gamble on advertising, I would rather reach out with a series of touches that are important to my clients and prospects. Strategic marketing is simply an example of working smarter.

Don't be scared off by a monthly mailing cost of $4.50 for each prospect. Focus on the return on your investment rather than the cost. And don't skimp on materials; use high-quality paper and printing. If you want to be a top-notch salesperson, then you need top-notch marketing materials.

In addition to mail, your business cards can also provide an opportunity for some shameless marketing. One inventive suggestion: head for your local bookstore and slide your cards into books that connect with your industry. Don't think this will work? Let me tell you a little story.

One of my sales students, Terry, is a financial planner in Dallas. I told Terry that we were going to have a special sales session to celebrate his birthday, and we headed over to a local bookstore to buy him a couple of sales books. As we drove away from his office, I asked, "Terry, do you have some business cards with you?" He replied no. (*Major* sales violation. Always carry business cards with you!) I turned the car around and told Terry to grab about 30 cards. Then we resumed our route to the bookstore. I treated Terry to a cup of coffee and we headed over to the section on finance.

"Terry, do you have those business cards?"

"Yes."

"Good. Put one inside each of these books."

Blank stare. "Aren't we going to be thrown out of here?"

"No. And even if they do ask us to leave, so what? We'll drive to the other bookstore down the street."

With that, Terry nervously slipped his cards into the books.

Now for weeks prior to this, Terry had been planning an information seminar to introduce a financial services product. The venue was a swank country club in a Dallas suburb. Including purchasing invitations, hiring a telemarketing company, and the hosting and catering expenses, Terry spent $4,000 to $5,000 on the evening. He asked me to come and I arrived at the country club the night of the session—which was only a few days after our bookstore adventure—to find that Terry's sales manager was waiting at the door for me.

"Did you hear what happened?" he asked.

"No."

"You're not going to believe this. Terry got a call from a man needing to invest about $50,000! He was in the bookstore looking at books on investing and, by the grace of God, Terry's card dropped out of one. He's here tonight!"

Not including support staff and other financial planners, maybe three or four people—plus the man from the bookstore—showed up for the seminar. No one did business with Terry that night . . . except the man who found Terry's card in a book. And he, of course, invested $50,000.

Another important aspect of a successful T.O.M.A. campaign is to incorporate social media. As a salesman, however, I prefer to call it **social *sales* media**. All of the social networking sites—Facebook, LinkedIn, Twitter, YouTube, MySpace, Plaxo—should be used by salespeople and sales organizations to generate business, *not* to socialize. We F.O.Ns are on a mission, and we need to stay focused on that mission—even when we're utilizing social *sales* media.

The first social networking site known to businesspeople was the local Chamber of Commerce meeting. Two groups of people attended these meetings. The first was made up of business owners and salespeople who came to visit with one another. They collected business cards from other chamber members and then promptly threw the cards away when they returned to their offices. The other group—and, in my observation, the smaller of the two—was composed of disciplined salespeople who came to the meetings to mine information and *actually close* business.

I don't often attend Chamber of Commerce meetings; however, I make a point of having "significant conversations" when I do. At one particular meeting of about 60 business people, I conversed with six people and collected business cards, birth dates, hobbies, and sales challenges from each, all in the span of about 30 minutes. By four o'clock that afternoon, I was on my way to the post office with six pink envelopes that contained copies of *Sales Mastery Book of Quotes*, my own compilation of inspirational quotes and business tips. Over the next four weeks, those six people received four mailings. In addition, eight e-mails were sent automatically at predetermined dates and times over the succeeding eight months. That's a total of 24 mailings and 48 e-mail touches. Plus, everyone's name and personal data was logged into Outlook and iContact. How many of the other 60 people at that meeting do you think bothered to follow up with the people they met? If you participate in meetings like these but are failing to gain revenue from them, then either stop attending or change your sales process at those gatherings so that you *do* generate business. (See Figure 2.4.)

The same discipline also applies to online social *sales* media. Do you and your company need a presence in the various social *sales* media? Absolutely! Should you use social *sales* media to socialize rather than sell? Definitely not, unless you're okay with being mediocre (in which case, this book will do nothing more than become a decorative piece on your bookshelf). You would be wise to take a hard look at your social networking activities and eliminate those that steal you away from time spent producing revenue.

Be wary as well of so-called social networking experts. Do these self-proclaimed specialists have a solid track record of producing

Introducing...
Social Media Branding

Social Media (SM) sites are growing more and more popular each year! Don't miss out on the opportunity to keep your name in front of your clients and keep up with them.

Stand out. Speak Up.
Get Branded.   More Info

www.chuckbauer.com • www.cbsalestools.com

FIGURE 2.4

business for salespeople, or are they trying to revamp a struggling consulting business while driving a car that's missing a hubcap? They blog about selling, but are they actually bringing in revenue from making a sale? Check before you buy, and *always* track revenue results earned from social *sales* media to know whether or not you should be spending less time online and more time focused on other areas of T.O.M.A.

Your T.O.M.A. campaign will net results, but only if you commit the time necessary at the start. The Time and Money Chart in Figure 2.5 illustrates the correlation between time spent on a T.O.M.A. campaign and dollars earned. As you can see, the first month will require the most time, and result in the least amount of money. As more time passes, however, your T.O.M.A. campaign will demand less of your time and provide increasingly greater income. By the end of the fifth or sixth month, there will be a noticeable

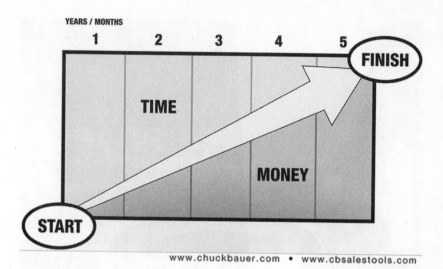

www.chuckbauer.com • www.cbsalestools.com

FIGURE 2.5

difference between time spent on your T.O.M.A. and the money you make.

Thus the front end of your T.O.M.A. campaign will take more time and effort, but the results will come. I call this the "vegetable mentality." Will eating vegetables for just a day give you any healthy benefits? No. If, however, you eat vegetables over an extended period of time, then of course you'll be healthier. Adapt this health-building idea for your T.O.M.A. campaign, and you will achieve sales benefits.

The Suspense Is Killing Me

Another important aspect of Marketing Yourself Shamelessly is creating *anticipation*. As a salesperson, you must use anticipation to your advantage with clients. There is no one who understood anticipation better than film director Alfred Hitchcock. Commenting about his films, Hitchcock said, "There's no terror in the bang, only in the anticipation of it." (See Figure 2.6.)

"There is no terror in the bang ... only in the **anticipation** of it."

~Alfred Hitchcock

www.chuckbauer.com • www.cbsalestools.com

FIGURE 2.6

Like Hitchcock, a salesperson should not divulge too much information too quickly. Relay only a few facts to excite customers, but withhold some to engage their curiosity. Whether you are communicating by phone, e-mail, or face-to-face, once you pull the trigger—once they hear the bang—there's nothing left.

Anticipation is an extremely powerful sales tool. In researching the subject online, I discovered a *Harvard Medical Journal* article that explains how anticipation plays a powerful role in—and has an intense effect on—memory. When applied to the Marketing Yourself Shamelessly principles, anticipation's role in memory allows each touch—whether by mail, e-mail, phone, or face-to-face—to deepen your clients' awareness of you and your product or service. Layer by layer, you imprint your presence and your purpose into their memories. Anticipation's effect intensifies when your clients begin to look forward to your next correspondence. They wonder, "What's arriving next?" My students tell me that their clients thank them for always staying in touch. Take action, and use the power of anticipation as you Market Yourself Shamelessly to clients and prospects.

Marketing Yourself Shamelessly Commission Development Quiz

Anything fewer than 100 percent correct answers requires immediate additional work!

1. The six rules of effective T.O.M.A. are:
   A. You must be _____ (do not fear pink).

   B. "Don't overthink the think; _____."
      (sound familiar?)

   C. Only after _____ to _____
      touches do you begin to penetrate your client's conscience.

   D. "Do the work _____ time and forget about it." (If you're analytical, it's more than zero, less than two, and is an integer.)

   E. "If everyone else is doing it, _____-TOP!"

   F. Don't be _____! (rhymes with hazy)

2. The five stages of T.O.M.A. are:
   A. Add _____ to Outlook.
      (Regardless of title or importance)

   B. Immediately send to the client the _____
      _____ book

   C. Send distinctive and staggered _____
      pieces (not e-mail).

   D. Send also distinctive and staggered _____
      pieces (rhymes with female).

   E. Use a service like _____ to
      issue a quarterly newsletter.

(continued)

(*Continued*)

3. What color, if used in your marketing pieces, will induce drowsiness? _____

4. _____ is the greatest client management tool known to man if maximized, because it will buy back time for you and will create revenue by helping you to close more business!

5. Besides colored envelopes and postage stamps, what expensive office tool will help you manage your T.O.M.A. campaign more precisely?

6. Again, do the work _____ time(s). (a) 25 (b) 100 (c) 1
BONUS QUESTION! Just doing the T.O.M.A. on a few clients is being lazy. Sales Coach Chuck says "Mass action equals _____!"

Marketing Yourself Shamelessly Quiz Answers

1. A. Courageous
   B. Overdo the do
   C. 6-to-8
   D. One
   E. S
   F. Lazy

2. A. Everyone
   B. *Excerpts from the Treasury of Quotes*
   C. Mail

(*continued*)

(Continued)

    D. E-mail

    E. iContact

3. White

4. Outlook

5. Accordion file

6. One

BONUS ANSWER: Mass results.

CHAPTER

3

Personality Selling

I am a hired assassin. I set my target, I focus, I aim, and then I shoot. Shoot to sell.

That's how many of my colleagues describe my understanding of personality styles—and how vital that knowledge is to closing a sale. I must admit, however, that I was extremely skeptical about this tactic as it relates to selling early in my sales career.

While I toured the country speaking on behalf of The People's Network, I had the pleasure of hearing Dr. Tony Alessandra, an author and speaker noted for his expertise in the psychology behind personalities. Tony and I were on the same speaking circuit, and I frequently heard his one-hour presentation on the role that personalities play in relationships. To be honest, it sounded like a lot of psycho-mumbo-jumbo at first. But as I began to think about the information more carefully—and began to observe the psychology between two people in a sales process more closely—I realized that Tony was speaking the truth.

Encouraged by my newfound appreciation for this field, I began taking courses to learn about personality traits and types, including well-known curriculums offered by Myers-Briggs, BrainStyles™, DISC®, and McQuaig. While completing these courses, however, I began to see there wasn't a program that was structured specifically for sales. For that reason, I worked diligently for two years to create Personality Selling, a program that allows me to teach salespeople the skills they need to recognize clients' personality styles and, most importantly, to *close sales*!

Each individual has his or her own personality style, and is most comfortable communicating in accordance with that style. However, every salesperson—regardless of their personality—must accommodate his *client's or prospect's* personality style in order to close a sale. Different clients, of course, require different approaches. The Personality Selling system will enable you to close sales that you otherwise might have lost because of your inability to identify with personalities that are different from your own. While you can always continue to sell the way you have in the past and hope for another outcome, remember the saying attributed to Albert Einstein: "The definition of insanity is doing the same thing over and over again and expecting different results." Using the information provided in this chapter, you will be able to achieve real, moneymaking results.

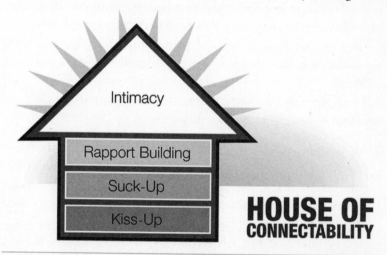

www.chuckbauer.com • www.cbsalestools.com

FIGURE 3.1

There are three benefits to Personality Selling. First, you will work *smarter* rather than *harder*. Second, you will build intimacy—and not just rapport—with your clients. You'll see in the three-story House of Connectability (Figure 3.1) how most salespeople remain on the first two floors of "kiss-up" and "suck-up." Some manage to climb to "rapport-building," which is as far as other sales programs go. Personality Selling, however, will allow you to move beyond rapport and toward *intimacy*—more valuable in sales because it eliminates your clients' fear, uncertainty, and doubt. Once you've "cleared the F.U.D.," then closing sales is easy. The third thing that Personality Selling allows you to do is distinguish yourself in yet another way from your villainous competitors. Even if they've read about personality styles, chances are that the material was not geared toward sales. Though Personality Selling is designed to enhance your professional skills, don't be surprised when you find yourself using this knowledge to improve your personal relationships as well.

This chapter is primarily based on the research and writings of psychologist Dr. William Moulton Marston, a great mind of the early twentieth century. Marston's quadrant behavior model identifies four main personality styles and his supporting work exhibits specific characteristics common to each particular style. Each quadrant identifies individuals' relative propensity to behave according to a predictive scale...making practical mind reading a very real possibility!

The following five behavior statements comprise the platform of Personality Selling's key sales tactics:

1. **All people can be motivated.** While many make the claim that some people just cannot be motivated, I don't think that's true. As I tell sales managers, you need to know what makes a salesperson tick, and you also need to know what ticks them off. There are two sides to every coin. The same applies to salespeople; find out what makes your prospects "tick," and find out what their hot-button issues are, as well.

2. **People do things for their own reasons.** If we give people a reason that is meaningful to them, then we can motivate them.

The challenge is that most salespeople come off as self-serving, versus interested in serving the prospect or client. Salespeople need to show their clients that they truly *care* about them and their reasons for being interested in a particular product or service. The flip side of this is that the salespersons' only interest is in closing the deal and making a commission.

3. **An overextension of a person's strength becomes a weakness.** Let's consider, for example, an analytical salesperson's probable selling process. As the sale begins to close, the prospect says, "Great! I love the product. I'm ready to buy—here's my payment in cash." The analytical salesperson, who wants the customer to know all the information available about a product before buying, says something like, "Wait a minute! I'm not done. I need to tell you about all the other advantages of this product." Then the sale pitch continues when it should have ended when the prospect was ready to pay. In instances like this, analytical salespeople sometimes manage to talk themselves out of a sale, thus turning their strength into a weakness.

4. **If I understand you better than you understand me, then I can control our communication.** In other words, salespeople who understand their prospects better than their prospects understand them will be able to persuade prospects to return phone calls and e-mails, respond to mail, and connect face-to-face.

5. **If I understand you better than you understand you, then I can control you.** Don't think of control in this case as manipulation. As a person of integrity, you are not attempting to manipulate a prospect. As a salesperson, however, you are a professional persuader; that's simply what you're hired to do. Your job really begins when a prospect says, "No." Understanding your prospect is the first step you must take in order to change that "No" to a "Yes."

With these five factors in mind, let's study the four types of personality styles and discover how this knowledge will increase your revenue. (See Figure 3.2.)

www.chuckbauer.com • www.cbsalestools.com

FIGURE 3.2

The Four Personality Styles

Although the names may differ from program to program, psychology generally recognizes four types of personalities. For sales purposes, the names of the four types indicate the dominant personality trait of any client or prospect.

Directors are authoritative.

Socializers are gregarious.

Relaters identify with everybody.

Thinkers are logical and analytical.

Remember the acronym: D.S.R.T. Once you've determined a prospect's personality type, input one of these letters into your follow-up information—whether on paper, on your iPad, or in Outlook. Then, when contacting this person in the future, you will not only know with *whom* you are dealing, but *what*.

Personality styles are recognizable among the world's rich and famous. One example would be President George W. Bush. Another would be George Steinbrenner, who was the principal owner of the New York Yankees until his recent death. They were both *directors*. British businessman Sir Richard Branson, best known for his Virgin brand of companies, including Virgin Records and Virgin Atlantic Airways, is a great example of a *socializer*; he runs his companies like one big ongoing party. Before her untimely death in 1997, Princess Diana was a highly *social* person. Talk-show host Oprah Winfrey and former secretary-general of the United Nations Kofi Annan are both outstanding *relaters*. Mozart was not only a renowned classical composer, but also highly regarded as a *thinker* in his time. Currently, we can look to former Federal Reserve chairman Alan Greenspan as an example of a gifted *thinker*.

Personality is dictated by the brain, which is divided into two hemispheres, the left and the right. Socializers and relaters predominantly use the right side of the brain: the seat of emotion, feelings, and imagination. Directors and thinkers are left-brain-based, and are therefore guided by ego and logic. Thus a person's words and actions are usually controlled by either feelings or ego.

As you determine your client's or prospect's personality, your interactions with them should follow their preference for the left or right brain. In a face-to-face situation, left-brain people want a handshake, while people who are right-brain dominant would prefer a hug. When you are meeting with a client who is a director or a thinker—those who are mostly guided by the left brain—sit across from them, with a conference table or desk between the two of you. On the other hand, if you are working with a right-brained individual such as a socializer or relater, move your chair around the desk so that you are seated side-by-side.

Another important point to remember is that left-brain people tend to say, "I think" when beginning an opinion, while right-brain people say, "I feel." It works to your advantage to be able to match their preference. When a person senses that someone else is communicating with them using their style, they're more likely to begin building rapport, and are on the verge of gaining intimacy. This, of course, moves you toward closing the sale. If you are presenting to a group, then you are likely to be addressing both right-and left-brain people, and will therefore need to connect with both. During my workshops, I often use the words *think* and *feel* in the same sentence to appeal to both types of groups.

Last but not least among the differences between right-and left-brain preferences, the feelings-based socializers and relaters tend to *ask* people what to do; the ego-based directors and thinkers *tell* people what to do. Unless, of course, the socializers are late for a party; then they tell everyone what to do!

If you're thinking that most people are a blend of left- and right-brain personalities—sometimes they're directors and sometimes they're relaters—then you're right. All humans are a mix of the four personality types to some degree. However, in times of conflict or stress—and even during a sale—people tend to revert back to the God-given, dominant personality they've had since the day they were born.

All of which begs the question: how can I identify my client's dominant personality style? There are four little words—whether spoken on the phone, typed in an e-mail, or spouted in your office or during a presentation—that serve as a lasso of truth. Once you've broken the ice and begun to form an amiable relationship with a prospect, simply say: *Tell me about you.*

This top-secret question, as I like to call it, is completely neutral. It does not hijack the answer and direct it to the left or right side of the brain. After a few minutes of pleasant conversation and questioning your client's needs and challenges, you might say, "Do me a favor—tell me about you." This phrase allows the person to whom you're speaking to formulate a response based on his or her personality style. Do not say, "Tell me about you *personally*," or "Tell me about you *professionally*." Neither of those inquiries is neutral. Once you've asked the question—then be quiet and listen. Chances are you'll know the client's dominant personality style within the first 10 words of a response.

Directors, socializers, relaters, and thinkers will all have their own unique reply this request. Use your highly tuned sales ear to hear what they're *really* saying, and that sensitive sales nose to sniff out the true meaning. In general, *directors will have an ego-based response*, such as "My business is great," "I caught the biggest fish," "I have 15 plaques on my wall," "I have the most to lose," or "I've been doing this for 10 years." The statement comes from the ego, or the left side of the brain.

Socializers will tend say something about family. I once met a woman at a Nationwide Financial sales event in Denver where I was presenting my course Marketing Yourself Shamelessly. This woman looked and behaved very professionally; when she spoke to the audience, she came across as knowledgeable and prepared. I visited with her during a break and said, "Do me a favor. Tell me about you." She immediately started talking about her cute little twin boys, one of whom had recently been hospitalized for a lung infection, but who was thankfully doing okay. For the next five minutes, this decidedly professional woman talked about her family. Because I kept the question neutral, she gave me an answer that was right-brain generated. Based on her responses, I knew immediately that she was right brain dominant, so her dominant was socializer followed by her secondary which was director.

When relaters hear "Tell me about you," they typically become silent for a few moments because they are processing the question. They tend to deflect the question back to *you*, saying, "Tell me about you first," *because relaters do not want to be in the spotlight*. In fact, they're afraid that you'll push them to talk about themselves. So talk about yourself; a relater truly wants to know about you.

Thinkers immediately make their personality style known visually and audibly. When you say, "Tell me about you," thinkers will usually fold their arms, bring a finger up to their face, their eyes will roll up to the left and they'll be silent for a few seconds. Then they'll look at you and respond, "That's kind of an interesting question. Why are you asking?" I advise salespeople to answer the question accurately and authentically. State that you are trying to determine more about their personality in order to interact according to their communication preferences.

Closing the Sale According to Personality Style

If trying to fight a fire, do you blow wind at it? I hope not. If trying to fight wind, do you throw dirt at it? Not unless you want dirt thrown back at you! Likewise, you must understand how to approach each one of your clients. With experience, practice, and implementation, you will know how to accommodate your clients' personalities in order to guarantee a sale.

Once you determine your client or prospect's personality style, closing becomes merely a matter of procedure.

Directors

The most important step when closing with directors is to remember to always give them two options. Directors are control freaks; a choice between two options makes them safe. If they're only given one option, they feel as though they're being hustled, which generates resistance that in some cases will kill the sale. Even if the second alternative essentially offers the same advantages as the first, you remove their fear by providing two choices instead of one.

Make sure that you're always focused, prepared, and organized when closing with a director. Have facts to back up the information you provide. Explore the results of your product or offering, but keep an eye on the clock as you do so, because time is of the essence to a director. Pay them only one compliment; more than that, and a director will think you are a weak suck-up.

Directors like to be in charge, so let them take the lead in a closing. How? Pitch them on three features of your product or service and then ask them to recite the information back to you. Say, "Go ahead, pitch that back to me. Sell *me* on it."

Sometimes director types will play games with you just to see your reaction. They might not show up for an appointment or may put you off repeatedly. If you overreact, then you lose; underreact and you win. Be strong—or as I like to say, "Bust them elegantly on their bulls—t and tell them to stop their silly behavior." Communicate that you have a request, and then firmly state it: "Stop giving me the same objection over and over" or "Stop making me jump through hoops" or "Stop making me try to overreact to you." Sometimes directors don't even realize they are playing games.

Socializers

Closing for socializers is an assumption that should feel like a spontaneous decision. You must presume the close with them; make it a "we/us"-based decision. Say something like "*Let's* go ahead and get this business done. You'll be glad that you did. You'll wake up tomorrow morning extremely happy that you made this choice." You've got to put your arm around socializers or give them a slight shoulder tap and help them make that spontaneous decision. Additionally, the decision *must* enhance their status in their community of family and friends.

In addition to spontaneity, socializers need enthusiasm. Let them set the pace, but be animated. Think of something that excited you and transfer that feeling to your socializer. Explore their dreams. Tell personal stories. Offer an incentive to purchase. Spotlight their uniqueness. Emphasize how purchasing your product, offering, or service will enhance their status.

Relaters

There are two words that must come out of your mouth when closing relaters: guarantee *and* assurance. For example, you might say, "I would like to read this guarantee for you." Once you've read this promise out loud, give them a bit of a hug or a shoulder tap, and say, "I give you my *personal assurance* on everything I just told you." Once you've given them the guarantee and assurance, you're on your way to closing the sale.

Do not, however, use formalities and official designations when selling to relaters; instead, be warm and informal. Explore their work and their specific needs. Instead of closed questions that merely call for "yes" or "no" answers, use open-ended questions that require discussion. A great test question to ask a relater is "How do you feel about it?"

Always emphasize harmony, safety, and teamwork with relaters. Like socializers, relaters need to feel that you are making the decision *with them*. Therefore, you must provide direction and assurance.

One of my students once asked for my advice on dealing with a client who was resisting a sale. I asked her the two questions I ask any student asking for help: (1) Have you sent Jim Rohn's book, *Excerpts from the Treasury of Quotes*, to create a positive first impression? and (2) Do you know the client's personality style? She answered "yes" to both questions, and added, "She is a relater." My student also knew that the client was shopping some competing salespeople and their companies. I reviewed the e-mails between my student and the client, and advised her to restructure the communication in the following ways: eliminate the official designations and make the e-mail more informal, drop the legalese, and, last but not least, restate the guarantee on your product and give the prospect your personal assurance. Two hours later, my student called to let me know that she had closed the deal.

Thinkers

The one detail to remember when closing sales with thinkers *is that they will not make a decision until they know the worst-case scenario.* You must discuss the negatives up-front with thinkers, because that's what they're looking for. Thinkers automatically default to disaster. Therefore, let them work out what might be their worst possible outcome. Beware of the voice in your head telling you not to talk about negatives; this normally kills the deal. That is sales immaturity, whereas giving thinkers the worst-case scenario requires sales maturity. However, should you discuss negatives with directors, socializers, or relaters? Absolutely not.

Another point to keep in mind when closing thinkers is to *avoid social talk*. Thinkers want more time to think. In fact, when they say, "I need to think about it," they really *do* need to think about it—because they are trying to imagine that worst-case scenario. Use this as an opportunity to explore their expertise, objectives, and concerns. Don't ask long, laborious questions. Instead, ask closed-ended questions that require only yes or no answers. Document the options that you give thinkers in order to emphasize your (and your products' or service's) accuracy and reliability. To understand how closings with the four personality types should be conducted, consider the Cups of Knowledge in Figure 3.3.

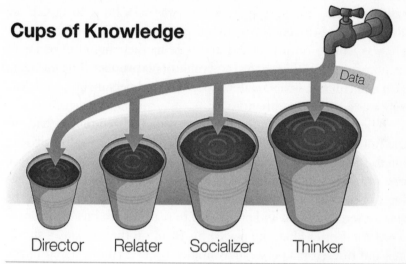

Cups of Knowledge

Director   Relater   Socializer   Thinker

www.chuckbauer.com • www.cbsalestools.com

FIGURE 3.3

Satisfying each personality type requires different amounts of information. As shown in the diagram, the director has the smallest cup, a relater's cup is slightly larger, the socializer needs a bit more information, and the thinker has the largest cup. *Once you determine a client or prospect's personality type, deliver as much information as necessary to fill his or her cup—and then stop the data flow and ask for the order.* Don't light a match with a flamethrower. The challenge that most salespeople face is that they tend to overfill a client's cup and give more information than the client wants or needs.

Closing Sales with Clients Who Present Different Personality Styles

What if you encounter a client meeting wherein you are dealing with two individuals who have different personality styles? How do you close the sale? You cater to both personalities. Consider what happened to Bob Meyers, a Sales Tune-Up client of mine in Denver, Colorado. Bob sells a household-cleaning appliance. We had spent one day on sales training, and the next day making sales calls together. The last appointment was scheduled to take place after Bob had driven me to the airport to catch my flight home. He was calling on a husband and wife in their home in order to demonstrate the effectiveness and value of his product. The husband, Bob determined, was a relater/feelings-based personality, while the wife was a socializer/director.

Before asking them for the order, Bob realized that he had left the notes on closing different personalities in his car after driving me to the airport. He excused himself and ran out to double-check the strategies on closing a relater and a socializer. Upon returning to the customers' living room, Bob deliberately sat next to the relater-style husband and proceeded to read his product's guarantee word-for-word. Then, he placed his hand on the husband's shoulder and offered his personal assurance on everything stated in the guarantee. The husband then stated "I'm sold on the system." Then Bob turned to the socializer-style wife and said, "Why don't I order a pizza and we can finish the paperwork while we're eating?" What an incentive! Bob closed both the husband and the wife by communicating according to each one's respective personality styles.

Quick Tips for Closing the Sale with Each Personality Type

Give directors two options.

Give socializers an incentive to buy and assume the close with them.

Give relaters a guarantee and your personal assurance.

Give thinkers the worst-case scenario.

What the Four Personality Types
Really Want to Know

Be prepared to answer the client's questions even before they ask as you close a sale with each personality type. **Among directors,** who base their perspective on ego and logic, **the primary question is** "What . . . ?" What is the product? What does it cost? What happens next? If you are getting resistance from a client who is a director, chances are you haven't answered all of the "What?" questions regarding your product or service.

Socializers want to know "Who?" Who is behind the product you're selling? As a salesperson, don't make the mistake of not acknowledging the company and all of the people backing you.

Relaters tend to ask "Why?" Why are we conducting the sale this way, and why not that way? You'll need to explain your reasons to a relater.

Finally, **thinkers are primarily interested in "How?"** How does the product work? How will it ship? How will you work out the details of the service? To close a sale with a thinker, be certain to have answers ready for all of the possible "How?" questions.

Aside from wanting to have the answers to different kinds of questions, the four personalities display varying strengths and weaknesses that provide insight into how you can successfully close a sale with them. We already know that directors' strength is that they are leaders. Their weakness, however, is impatience. As a result, directors are decisive; once they arrive at a decision, that's it—there's no turning back.

Despite their decisiveness, directors fear they will be hustled. To that end, be sure that you provide your own and your company's track record. Directors achieve a higher level of satisfaction once they know that your personal history—and that of the company you represent—is solid.

The strong suit of socializers is persuasion, while their weakness is disorganization. In fact, I can frequently pick out the socializers when I'm speaking to an audience; they are the people who don't wear watches. They make decisions spontaneously, but they fear rejection. Make this fear part of your closing tactic with socializers. For example, you might tell socializers that if they don't meet certain qualifications, they could be rejected from your program. Anxiety about such rejection—and a sense that their status will be enhanced if they purchase your company's product—will move socializers closer to the sale.

You can pull a socializer even closer to the sale with incentives. Maybe this means taking them to dinner, offering them a gift coupon, or shipping a pizza—even if they're hundreds of miles away. Furthermore, socializers are most satisfied through regular contact and communication with a salesperson. If you stop all forms of communication with a socializer after the close, then you will lose getting referrals from that person. So don't be lazy; maintain a connection with a socializer, as you should with all clients!

The strength among relaters is listening, and the weakness is indecisiveness. Relaters are the best listeners on earth, but tend to have a lot of trouble making decisions. A conversation between two relaters might go something like this:

"Hey, let's go to dinner."

"Yeah, where do you want to go?"

"I don't know. Where do you want to go?"

"I don't know."

"Are you sure you really want to have dinner?"

Their decision—when it finally happens—is based on togetherness. Like socializers, relaters are motivated by words such as *we* and *us*. Therefore, always keep in mind when closing a sale with a relater that you are making the decision *together*. And again, like socializers, relaters need regular, ongoing contact and communication. Without this, you lose them as a referral base, because they feel you have broken an intimate connection.

Lastly, relaters fear sudden change. Therefore, salespeople must answer all questions they have regarding how a decision will affect them personally. Remember: relaters need a guarantee and your personal assurance.

Thinkers' strength is organization, but their weakness is perfectionism. Thinkers are often so consumed with perfection that they overlook experiences and miss out on great communication. Their decisions are deliberate and a long time coming, because they fear making a mistake and being criticized for doing so. With this in mind, sales presentations to thinkers need to reaffirm that their decision is mistake-and-criticism-free. Thinkers must be able to justify a decision logically; therefore, data, documentation, timetables, and ultimately clarity in a sales presentation are critical.

Finally, let's consider the overall prevalence of each personality type within the U.S. population. Directors comprise approximately 15 percent; socializers make up another 15 percent, relaters represent the majority of the population at 60 percent (although as salespeople we don't run into them as often as their numbers would indicate, since they are typically not company decision-makers), and thinkers constitute 10 percent. Thus, *the personality styles of some 75 percent of the population are* feeling and right-brain-based, *while 25 percent are* ego, logic, and left-brain-based.

This information not only supports how vital it is to understand a client's personality style in closing a sale; it also becomes crucial in sales marketing as well. *In order to make the greatest impact, all of your marketing pieces should appeal to both left-and right-brain personality types.* In Chapter 5, where we'll cover Sales Tools, you will find out how various marketing pieces can be designed to appeal to directors and thinkers, socializers and relaters. In the meantime, let me leave you with the following story.

One of the marketing tools my company offers is the Fast Facts Profile, a one-page description of a salesperson that appeals to both right-and left-brain clients. Professional writers on my staff write these profiles to appeal to both sides of the brain. Likewise, the profile includes two photographs. One is a professional headshot, which appeals to the left brain, and the other is a casual, friendly shot, appealing to the right brain.

One of my students had her Fast Facts Profile lying on her desk when her sales manager walked into her office. Looking at the photos on the page—one in which the salesperson is suited up and the other while on vacation in a foreign country—the manager said, "You really need to remove that vacation shot. Nobody's going to like that picture." The sales manager, of course, was an ego-based left-brain personality. He assumed that the rest of the world thought in the same way he did, and could not imagine the appeal of a vacation photo. On the other hand, his salesperson fully understood the value of having two photos on her profile. She's a hired assassin . . . shooting to sell.

Personality Selling Commission Development Quiz

Anything fewer than 100 percent correct answers requires immediate additional work!

1. Which of these is a true statement?
   A. It's more effective selling to pitch someone the same way you would prefer to be pitched.

   B. Your competitors are very likely to already be implementing personality selling.

   C. By learning the personality styles, your revenue will decrease because it's replacing the time you use to reorganize your e-mail.

   D. Personality selling will blast you into the intimate zones (beyond rapport) to help you become a more efficient closer.

2. Number these items in the order in which they most often occur according to the House of Connectability.

   _____ Suck-up

   _____ Build rapport

   _____ Build intimacy

   _____ Kiss-up

   (continued)

(*Continued*)

3. Based on Marston's model, complete the following para-phrase: "If I understand you better than you understand me, then I can control the _____. I can make you respond to my voicemail, e-mail, face-to-face meetings..."

    A. Lunch hour

    B. Break room

    C. My coworkers

    D. Communication

4. Most important, Marston proposes that "If I understand you better than you understand _____, then I can control you."

5. Which two personality types reveal themselves by using the word "think"?

6. Which two personality types reveal themselves by using the word "feel"?

7. What is the memory-jogging acronym for the four main personality types?

8. How many words are in the top-secret question that will instantly determine your client's personality type? (a) 4 (b) 40 (c) 400

(*continued*)

(*Continued*)

9. Draw a line to connect the primary one-word closing question for each of the personality types:

Socializer	"What?"
Director	"Who?"
Relater	"How?"
Thinker	"Why?"

10. Which personality type fears any sudden changes?

11. Which personality type fears being hustled?

12. Which personality type fears rejection?

13. Which personality type fears criticism for any mistake?

14. In the situation of a director not making a decision, how do you get them "off the fence?"

15. How do you get a socializer off the fence?

16. How do you get a relater off the fence?

17. How about a thinker?

18. When Sales Coach Chuck is asked a question by one of his sales students, what are the first two questions he poses to the student before going any further into the conversation?

(*continued*)

(*Continued*)

Personality Selling Quiz Answers

1. D
2. 2, 3, 4, 1
3. D
4. Yourself
5. Director, Thinker
6. Socializer, Relater
7. DSRT
8. 4
9. Socializer: "Who?"
   Director: "What?"
   Relater: "Why?"
   Thinker: "How?"
10. Relater
11. Director
12. Socializer
13. Thinker
14. Present two options to a director
15. Offer incentives to a socializer
16. Offer personal assurances to a relater
17. Provide documentation to a thinker
18. (1) Did you send out the *Excerpts from the Treasury of Quotes* by Jim Rohn to create a positive first impression?
    (2) Do you know their personality type?

CHAPTER

4

Becoming a Sales S.T.U.D.

If you've never considered yourself to be a stud before, now's your chance. And you won't just be any kind of stud: you're going to be a *sales* S.T.U.D. (See Figure 4.1.)

S.T.U.D. is the acronym that I use for the four critical steps in a sales process which are overlooked by many salespeople around the world:

Specific next step

Takeaway

Urgency

Deadline

Specific Next Step

Whether your meeting is face-to-face or over the telephone, via e-mail, letter or text message, *any* communication with a client

FIGURE 4.1

http://www.chuckbauer.com/sales-seminars/

or prospect must end with a specifically designated next step. At the end of a conversation, most salespeople leave their clients in F.H.A.—fog, haze, and ambiguity. Establishing a decided-upon next step eliminates F.H.A. and brings the conversation to 100 percent completion. In other words, your work is done up to that point.

Of course, there is a wrong way and a right way to set up the next step. Consider the common approach to a typical sales phone call: many sales instructors tell their students to ask something such as, "Will Tuesday at two or three o'clock work for you, or does Wednesday at four work better?" You don't want to be the Maytag repairman, giving them the choice of all the open times you have available. There's a better way to go about this. When designating that specific next step, the better way is to not *ask*, but to *instruct*. Tell your clients or prospects when *you* are available and *then* proceed: "I've got Tuesday at three o'clock open. Will that work for you?" If they say yes, that's great; you're done for now. If they say no, then you move to another time that is open on *your* calendar. Cut the umbilical cord to the past sales culture in which catering to the client was widely believed to be the best thing for the client. Do you want the client to take your job? Probably not; so stop giving it to them. Keeping control of the professional situation is the best client service you can provide. **You must control the specific next step and the entire sales process.**

Whatever the specific next step—meeting, phone call, or letter—using Outlook is a must. Beyond the basic date, time, and location, Outlook provides space for a message in the body of the calendar invite, as well as a means to insert your signature. Once recipients' e-mail addresses are posted and the e-mail is sent, Outlook's real advantages will materialize. Clients and prospects can accept or decline the scheduled next step, propose a new time, or indicate that they have "tentatively" scheduled the appointment. When they accept—and most of the time, they will—Outlook propagates your prospects' calendars, sending e-mails back to you to indicate their acceptance. In other words, Outlook sends a reminder about having set an appointment. This saves a lot of time and reduces the number of ping-pong phone chats. (See Figure 4.2.)

Here's an illustration of the respect, efficiency, and positive response generated by this application: a student of mine performs the first steps in a sales process for a sales company. Strategic and calculated calls are placed to business owners who are not necessarily expecting her contact. Before ever speaking to one particular prospect, she sent an Outlook calendar invitation for a scheduled call, with a start time of 10:35 and end time adjusted to 10:45. In the message body, she writes: *I am a Senior Business Advisor with (company website stated). This call will be to discuss a business interest. If this time conflicts with your schedule, please respond with your next preference of either 1:10 or 3:40.*

At *exactly* 10:35, she places the call. Once connected to the owner, she reintroduces herself and comments that she wasn't certain whether or not the prospect has already seen her Outlook invitation. (Of course, she knows that the other person has seen it,

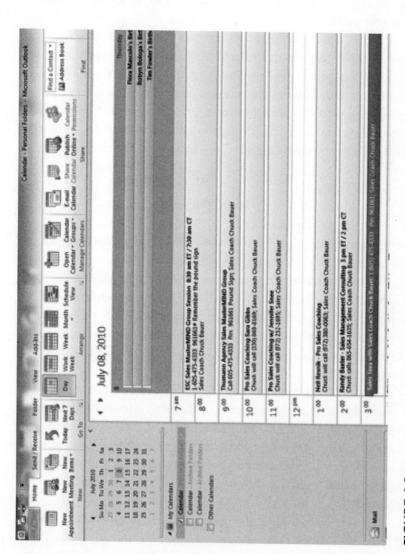

FIGURE 4.2

71

because she pre-sets all her Outlook correspondence with a "read receipt.") To that, he responds: *"Oh yes—and exactly on time. In fact, I was on another call when my reminder came up, and I had to end that call to take yours."*

Clients miss appointments for two major reasons: either the client doesn't respect the salesperson, or the salesperson is not practicing the precision-based sales tactics that Outlook offers. In fact, I recommend using commitment phraseology to remind clients of their obligation to show up for the appointment. Commitment can be defined as doing the thing you said you would do, long after the mood and emotion you were in when you said it has left you!

Takeaway

The second step toward becoming a Sales S.T.U.D. is to provide a sales takeaway. In the sales process, takeaway is all about psychology. Human nature dictates that we desire the most that which we cannot have. Sales psychology uses this desire to persuade people to do what they might not otherwise do. Freaks of Nature (F.O.N.s) understand this psychology and use it often, whereas others, like me, must learn it. Once understood, however, the psychology behind a takeaway is very powerful.

There is also what I call the Teeter-Totter effect. At one end of the teeter-totter there is exclusion, and at the other end is inclusion. Naturally, people want to be included. In the takeaway scenario, inclusion necessitates action. *First, a salesperson takes the product away; then a prospect must do something to warrant their having the product. Only after the prospect has done their part does the salesperson give the product back.*

There is both a hard and soft approach to takeaways. A hard takeaway uses bold language, a specific request, and deadlines. This type of takeaway is best used with the directors and thinkers personality styles. A soft takeaway that uses informal language and more nonchalant approaches works best with socializers and relaters. Again, you must use the right bait for the right fish.

However, both methods generate important discussions that will be the litmus tests as to whether a given product, service, or offering is right for a prospect.

John Pesuard is the salesman who taught me both techniques. John worked in Kentucky for a Dallas-based company selling business-advertising services. He was a master at the hard takeaway. Whenever he set an appointment, he would tell his prospect, "The only reason for this appointment is to determine whether or not you are qualified for our company's program. I can't sell you anything until we know that you are approved." This is how he dangled the product in front of prospects and persuaded them to "earn the right" to purchase. By making prospects worry that they might be excluded from his program, John required them to act in order to be included.

A salesperson might use the soft takeaway and say something such as, "Until you share more information with me about what your needs and challenges are, I'm not sure if my product or service is for you." For a prospect or client, this statement creates a psychological state in which there is an aversion to exclusion and a desire for inclusion. As a result, a prospect usually will provide the desired information.

For my own sales coaching consultancy, I use a takeaway. My Professional Sales Coaching program is extensive; it includes 18 sessions over six months, all of which are videotaped. I refuse to accept students who are not qualified for the program, because I must be able to project a successful outcome. I am paid very well to increase my clients' sales revenues and to advance their sales positions within their companies. Thus qualification is critical.

Typically, I have two interviews with a prospect to determine if they are the right kind of candidate for my coaching program. Many qualifications and soft takeaways are used in these discussions. Then, we discuss my fee. This is when I use a hard takeaway. Sometimes, candidates say, "Chuck, I'm ready to go. But I can't pay you the full amount. I can pay half now and half later." My response could be, "With respect, this isn't for you." At that moment, I've taken away the opportunity to use my service. When they ask why they are not qualified, I tell them the truth: after more than 20 years in sales and 17 years with my own sales training company, I know that people who are fully engaged—who have made the entire payment for my coaching program—do far better than people who want an installment plan. Without fail, candidates who initially don't have the money for the full payment will call back in a few days to tell me they do. In these cases, my takeaway worked. Truth + a Takeaway = Closing Super Power! Now I have a qualified student who is fully committed both financially and psychologically.

Consider which takeaway, soft or hard, will best serve you and the product or service you are selling. At the very least, you should be able to use a takeaway to generate more discussion. Stop for a moment right now and think of two takeaways that will work in your sales process. Write them down.

Urgency

Stop. Seriously. Did you write down your two takeaways first? Do these before you continue. What? No paper? What's this book page made of? Oh, sorry. No pen, you say. And you're in sales? Jot down those takeaways, and then continue.

When I think of urgency in sales, I remember the late Billy Mays, the television pitchman who sold OxiClean®, among other products. Mays exuded sales urgency with every word he spoke. "Wait! If you buy now, we'll include two for the price of one!" Am I suggesting that all salespeople talk and act like Billy Mays? No. But put your ego aside and realize that we can all learn a lesson from Billy: how to put urgency in our messages. The thought behind urgency is to "buy now" to avoid a price increase, to get a discount, or to begin installation. Can you find a reason for urgency in your own sales process?

One often-overlooked reason is the consequences prospects will face should they fail to purchase your product or service. Salespeople are so busy touting what a product will do for a prospect that they fail to mention the repercussions of *not* buying. "Listen, if you don't enroll in my underwater basket-weaving class, you're going to continue to experience the usual frustrations of bending branches while drowning." Consider demonstrating what clients will lack without your product.

Urgency also gives you the advantage of avoiding dreaded delayed decisions, which usually result in a client telling you "No." Don't give them wiggle room to say "I'll get back to you tomorrow." Allowing a delay gives the client time to find another salesperson—your competitor. Thus you must prevent delayed decisions in your sales processes. Urgency will help you overcome the delay factor.

In the end, your client or prospect has four choices when responding to a sales pitch:

1. Buy the salesperson's product, offer, or service.
2. Buy a competitor's (and make no mistake—every salesperson has competition.)
3. Take care of whatever their need is in their own way.
4. Do nothing.

Expressing a sense of urgency makes a prospect much more likely to buy. Without it, your sales process becomes what author and motivational speaker Zig Ziglar would call a "wandering generality." In essence, you become a wandering salesperson. Therefore, develop, create, and use urgency in your messages—and you'll make yet another sale.

When does the urgency start in a sales process? Why, that's easy—in the first 10 words out of your mouth. It's how you say it; does your prospect suspect that you are an "urgent" salesperson?

Deadline

The last letter of S.T.U.D. stands for deadline. In the sales process, deadlines serve to maintain the highest level of professionalism in communication because they eliminate the fog, haze, and ambiguity that I mentioned earlier. In short: **deadlines close business**. If you incorporate deadlines whenever you need a prospect or client to complete a task—especially a "closing" task—you move your sales skill level towards becoming a professional closer rather than a professional visitor.

Don't think people pay attention to deadlines? That's exactly the opinion voiced by an audience member during one of my seminars. I nearly laughed out loud at this, because it just so happened to be a seminar taking place in March—a mere month before the most recognizable enforced deadline in the United States. April 15th is the day on which income tax returns are due to the federal and state governments and the last day to postmark a return in order to avoid penalties. Drive by the post office in any American city at 9 P.M. on April 15th and you'll be likely to see a line of people in cars waiting to hand their returns to the postal worker standing outside. Believe me—salespeople who don't think deadlines work are the ones who let their ego or ignorance stand in the way of sales success.

Consider one of my students, who attended one of my MasterMIND teleclasses and who works for an oil and gas company in Houston, Texas. After learning the S.T.U.D principles, he decided to use them in an e-mail to a prospect. He also copied in his sales manager on the communication. The e-mail said:

> Although I haven't heard from you in quite awhile, I would like to re-introduce our solution to you. If you accept the offer by this Friday, then we will include free shipping on the oil and gas products you purchase. Again—the deadline for this offer is Friday. If I do not hear from you by then, I will cancel the offer.

All the elements of S.T.U.D—specific next step, takeaway, urgency, and deadline—are in that brief communication to the prospective client. The sales manager was not familiar with S.T.U.D. He rebuked the salesperson for being so bold as to tell a prospect what to do. However, the salesperson triumphed; he received an e-mail from the prospect that included a purchase order for $54,000, along with their documented desire to take advantage of the free shipping offer.

Another example of the effectiveness of S.T.U.D. occurred when I began working with a Fortune 100 company that makes thousands of outbound telephone sales calls each month. The sales staff pitched to business owners across the country and asked them to complete an application in order to enroll in a specific program. The applications were e-mailed to prospects, but very few were returned. From management's perspective, the unreturned applications meant that the calls were time wasted, not to mention lost revenue and misplaced potential profit.

Upon examining their sales processes, I immediately noticed that four important elements were missing: a specific next step, a takeaway, a sense of urgency, and a deadline. On calls, salespeople were timid, saying, "If you have a minute . . ." or "If you wouldn't mind filling out this application. . . ." There was nothing to indicate that this application *must* be completed—and soon.

Some time after I'd coached the sales team on the principles of S.T.U.D., Brandon, one of the company's young sales lions who was only in his mid-20s, wrote a four-sentence S.T.U.D. phrase similar to this:

> I have attached an application for the xyz program at Company ABC. This application is activated for 72 hours. If it is not returned within 72 hours, then I will need to secure an approval for extension. Contact me with any questions you may have.

Short, direct, and including all four elements of S.T.U.D.: Specific next step—complete the application. Takeaway—if it is not returned. Urgency—the application must be completed within 72 hours or an approved extension will be necessary. Deadline— 72 hours.

I also use S.T.U.D. principles when sending seminar proposals—which I prefer to call seminar solutions—to prospective clients. One that I recently completed was for a large bank in Dallas. I had previously worked with one of the bank's salespeople, helping her improve sales processes and increase revenue. This solution, however, was for a contract covering Sales Mastery coursework that I would present one day each month for a year at the corporate offices. My students at the bank would be an executive vice president, three executive vice presidents, and a sales division of 54 people. Despite the big bank image and the high-level executives involved, the solution included a specific next step, a takeaway, an element of urgency, and a deadline. We met on a Friday and I set the following Friday as the deadline for their response to the solution. After all, I've allocated time, resources, and my team's energy to the project; if we won't be going forward with the solution, then we need to know so that we can focus on other projects.

During that week, the executive vice president and I reviewed the solution. When we came to the one-week deadline, she explained that although it looked great, the president of the bank would need time to consider it as well. She asked for an extension of a week and I said "Yes." With clear communication—no F.H.A.—there was no reason to deny the deadline extension. And yes, the bank solution closed for a one-year sales consulting solution utilizing Sales Mastery.

Scheduling the specific next step is another time when it's absolutely necessary to use your Outlook calendar feature—especially when communicating any deadlines or client tasks (see Figure 4.3). Remember: *all* deadlines imposed on *any* prospects or clients should be communicated through Outlook's calendar feature. Additionally, the Outlook Calendar invite is essential when sending sales forms, applications, or proposals to prospects and clients. First, it propagates their calendars. From this point, Outlook automatically reminds them that the deadline is approaching (their Outlook is now working on my behalf), thereby eliminating any fog, haze, or ambiguity. Second, the system notifies me; now I know they've seen the e-mail and accepted the deadline. Outlook Calendar Invite keeps me—and will keep you—at the highest level of precision-based salesmanship.

Gone Fishin' (Bonus Sales Tactic!)

When communication with a client comes to a halt, Sales S.T.U.D.s go fishing (see Figure 4.4). Everyone in sales runs into roadblocks,

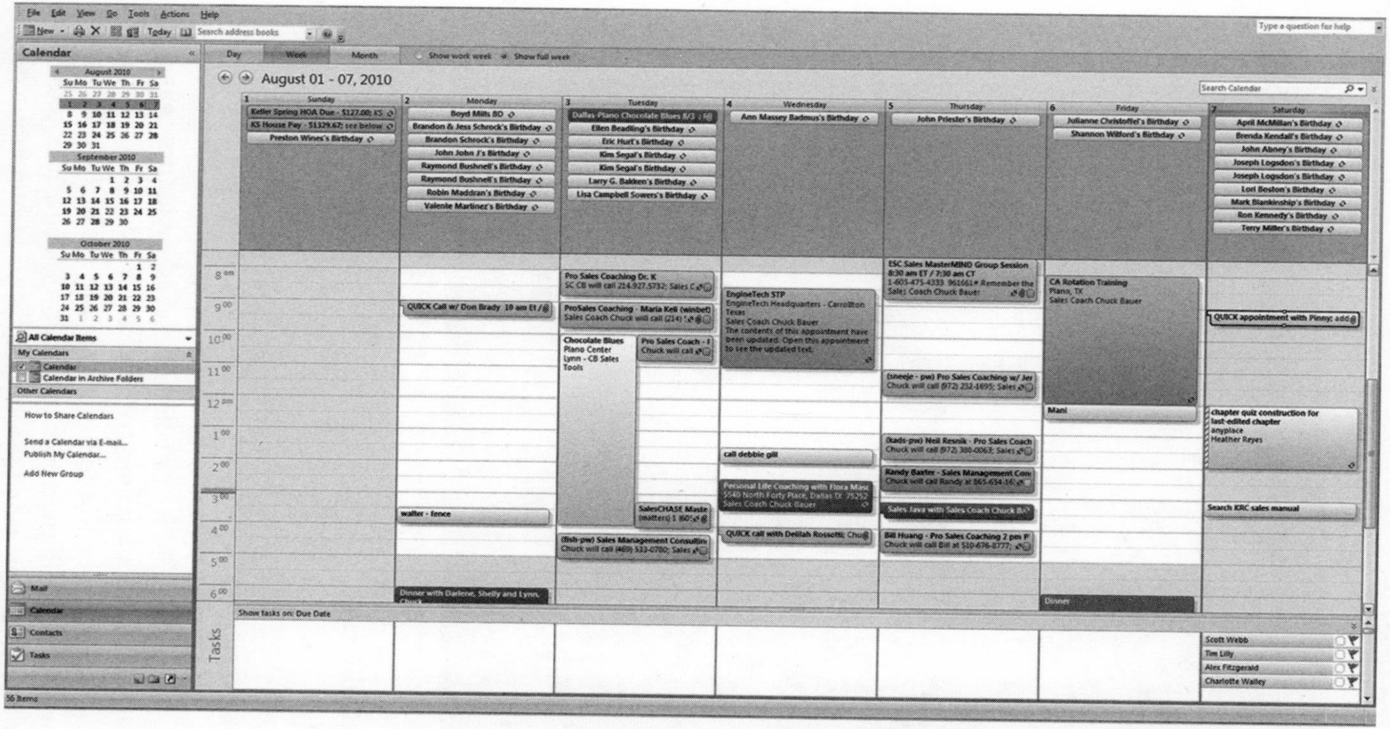

FIGURE 4.3

www.chuckbauer.com • www.cbsalestools.com

79

www.chuckbauer.com • www.cbsalestools.com

FIGURE 4.4

which are typically caused by dropped communication and hundreds of other things that most salespeople usually miss. A client stops e-mailing, stops responding to voice messages, or ignores our mail. That's when I tell my students to "fish" twice a day.

Everyone knows how to fish. Go out to a lake, bait the fishing line, throw the line in the water, and wait for a bite. The technique is essentially the same when fishing for clients hiding in the depths of lost communication. Throw out the bait twice a day and see if somebody bites.

1. When fishing for sales, first look for a prospect in your database who has stopped communicating with you. Maybe weeks if not months have passed since you last spoke to him or her. Next, go to your Outlook Calendar and pinpoint a time in the future—later today, sometime tomorrow—when you have a 15- to 30-minute time-block available. Open that block and on the subject line insert, "QUICK phone call with [prospect's name]." Capitalization of the word QUICK is critical and the reason is that your prospects all have three fears about you:

   1. You are selling something.

   2. You will waste their time.

   3. You will be just like all the other salespeople that they try to avoid.

That word QUICK coupled with a five-minute time-block in the Outlook calendar invite helps kill these fears before you ever get the prospect on the phone.

In the "location" field, type in your name and a message like this: "Brandon (the salesperson's name) will call (first name of prospect) at (prospect phone number) for a QUICK call." Because Outlook propagates appointments in 30-minute intervals, you will then need to manually adjust the time to a five-minute span in order to accurately indicate this will indeed be a *quick* call. Example: Call Start Time 3:00 P.M. CT. Call End Time 3:05 P.M. CT. Insert your signature in the body of the message, and then click Invite Attendees to add your prospect's e-mail address. Throw this bait out every day to two prospects or clients who have completely dropped communication.

You'll spend no more than a couple of minutes a day fishing, and will garner results far greater than those you might acquire from sending text messages every hour. Salespeople who regularly fish have a 20 to 50 percent success rate, which means that the client accepts the invitation and communication with the salesperson begins again. One of my sales coaching students tried the fishing technique on a client with whom he hadn't spoken in a very long time and received the following response:

> Joanna [the decision maker] is out of town, but I just spoke with her. She doesn't know who accepted the time you suggested, but unfortunately that will not work. Would next Wednesday at 9:00 A.M. fit your schedule? That would work best for us. Thanks. Have a wonderful day.

After months of no interaction, a single piece of bait comes back with a positive response—*and* "have a wonderful day!" Now *that* is a successful fishing trip.

Chasing versus Being Chased

As a salesperson, you are either chasing clients or clients are chasing you. There is no gray area where you're "mutually chasing" one another—and I learned early in my sales career that, unsurprisingly, being chased is *far* preferable. In my first couple of years selling cars for Nissan, I discovered that closing business with customers who were chasing me was much easier than closing with people I was chasing.

Salespeople who chase build codependent relationships with clients. And as any personal development coach or pastor would counsel, codependency is dysfunctional because one person is routinely sacrificing his or her needs for the needs of the other person in the relationship. If salespeople lack a basic level of skills or are not fully engaged—for example, when they neglect continuing sales education or are just plain lazy—many resort to forming codependent relationships with their prospects or clients. Unfortunately, that type of salesperson's income, no matter how good they think it is, is significantly meager. When closings do occur—and that is a rare event—it is because of an accident or happenstance, rather than skill.

Beware of chasing prospects and clients, or even giving that impression. Chasing clients puts them in control. Like a ringmaster at the circus, your client holds the hat, the whistle, and the hoop—and you're the one jumping through that hoop. Stop behaviors that diminish your level of professionalism; instead, make clients take you seriously.

For example, be careful about being overly nice. A nauseating number of "please" and "thank yous," incessant idle chitchat, and time wasted to curry the favor of prospects and clients is over the top. An approach like this actually reveals that a salesperson *lacks* advanced skills and sales maturity. If you asked prospects to number from 1 to 10 the key qualities they look for in the salespeople from whom they buy, do you think "being overly nice" would make the top 10? Nope, probably not.

Now, be careful here: I'm not telling you to be *mean*. What I *am* saying is that you can increase your sales skill levels by implementing the ideas from *Sales Mastery*. Work on becoming a *professional* salesperson/closer versus a codependent professional visitor with skinny kids who is consistently one to two weekly sales away from being asked to leave. That's being a sales *dud*! Remember—sales S.T.U.D.s pay attention to details, educate themselves, and do the hundreds of little things to *make* a prospect want to do business with them. It takes work—and it makes money!

Sales S.T.U.D.s are distinct—and there is absolutely no distinction in chasing. If you make phone calls, send e-mails, or schedule face-to-face meetings *ad nauseam*, then you are chasing prospects and clients just like almost every other salesperson. I give students in my one-on-one sales coaching program the following rule of thumb: **"Leave *one* voice message; send *one* e-mail."** If a client doesn't respond after that, then you must do something different; don't continue to leave unreturned messages and e-mails. Be distinct. Find a better and more creative way to get their attention. Phone messages and e-mails do not work en masse! And I'm certain that several of you who are reading this would like me to continuously spoon-feed you alternatives. But babying you in that way would forever keep you in diapers. I'll give you a little food, but you've got to activate your right brain to make your own feast.

When you chase clients, they sense desperation—which comes from fear. In sales, you are either fearful or confident. Repeatedly leaving phone messages and sending e-mails tells clients that you are desperate. You leave the impression that not only are you chasing, you are *begging* for business. Trade the time you spend chasing clients on sales *training* instead. Watch an online video that will nurture your sales persona. Work on the follow-up program laid out in Chapter 2: Marketing Yourself Shamelessly, log clients into Outlook and iContact, send the Jim Rohn book, and send staggered mail and e-mail. Remember the extraordinary numbers that Jeff Dunn posted after he received 190 leads: 3,420 touches over 12 months. *Do the work!* Become a precision-based salesperson. Remember, Outlook is the most efficient and therefore the best sales utilization tool known to man. Don't second-guess that by questioning whether or not clients use Outlook. You're even losing time and opportunity while you argue about it. Don't be . . . what? Lazy.

Salespeople who chase usually make the mistake of treating clients as if they are all the same. This couldn't be a less effective approach. Higher-level VIP clients and prospects must receive more indulgent treatment than clients who generate lower levels of revenue for you.

Ten Principles of Salespeople Who Are Chased

Let's conclude this discussion on becoming a Sales S.T.U.D. with the 10 principles that make a *salesperson* worth chasing.

1. **Approach prospects with a sales edge attitude**. Potential clients chase salespeople who have confidence to a degree that might easily be confused with having a pinch of arrogance: a touch of that "I-don't-care-if-you-do-business-with-me-or-not" attitude. This flips the sales psychology from "chasing

you" to "chasing me" and lets prospects and clients know that you are not willing to run after them. Don't forget—one phone call, one e-mail, and then move on to a different and more distinctive approach. (See Figure 4.5.)

FIGURE 4.5

2. **Schedule everything**—all prospect or client appointments and tasks. Nothing—not even a phone call—is left in a fog bank.

3. **Convey confidence**. Salespeople can have varying attitudes of confidence when it comes to approaching the sale: at one end of the spectrum is confidence, and at the other is fear. Your clients and prospects can sense immediately which end you're on. They want to work with salespeople who are confident, not fearful or timid. They are looking for reasons from the beginning to trust or distrust their salesperson. So—does your first impression set a tone of confidence and professional leadership? Or is it the babbling of a thumb-sucker? Remember: timid salespeople have skinny kids.

4. **Have—and continue to develop—a high level of skills**. Salespeople whom prospects chase are earning this status by

continuously working on their trade and seeking training to help them advance and refine their sales methods. Those who aren't doing these things are immobilized by the shackles of laziness around their lower-pay ankles.

5. **Have a set follow-up program** that works for you 24/7. Whether I'm in the gym or on vacation, whether the skies are clear or the barometric pressure is falling, my automated follow-up program is busy working. That reminds me—do you know what else I love about Outlook? It never asks for a raise or a benefits package. Outlook doesn't need to complete a lengthy employment application or pass a drug or lie-detector test—and it never steals money or asks for extra time off. The only agreement Outlook requires to work round-the-clock is that you keep your computer on. In that sense, Outlook is probably one of the best employees you'll ever have.

6. **Treat VIPs differently**. Salespeople who are chased treat clients in the top 20 percent of their database differently than those in the bottom 80 percent. VIPs deserve red-carpet treatment. One of my top revenue producers here in Dallas meets at least six of his VIPs each week for breakfast, lunch, or a visit to the local Starbucks just to stay in touch. The rest are touched via electronic means.

7. **Be precision-based**. So many sales people are continually behind the eight ball and are helter-skelter in their sales structure. Their follow-up is lackluster, and they spend too much time thinking and trying to make things perfect before starting. Have a *set* infrastructure and a set method of operation for all functions in your business. Stop having issues, laying blame, and justifying lackluster results. Start now and build a precision-based sales infrastructure. It starts with maximizing Outlook and using technology such as iContact and so forth.

8. **Understand the power of *not* becoming codependent**. Jeff Lang, the mortgage broker whom you met at the beginning of this book, initially came off as a desperate yes-man when he

began selling. He answered every phone call by the middle of the first ring, so excited to get a call that he was almost huffing and puffing. Now, Jeff allows voicemail to pick up every call. Codependent salespeople also tend to have multiple phone numbers on their nondistinct business cards. Come on; don't you think three or four phone numbers is a little over the top? I have heard some salespeople tell prospects that they can "call me whenever; call me late at night"! *Dysfunctional!* The better option is to declare specific communication boundaries with your prospects. Implement a prioritization system so that even if they have a sales emergency, they still get in touch with you in a way that keeps you in control of the communication. And here's a novel idea: answer the phone at *your* convenience.

9. **Stay in control**. If you want prospects and clients to chase you, then you must control the sales process and communication. Don't even *think* of stooping low enough to jump through the ringmaster's carnival hoop. One way to stay in control is to learn the value of telling clients "No." "No," you say? "NO!" could be your most powerful super-word.

10. **Ask for referrals**. Salespeople who are chased have an established referral response program. They have set policies and procedures that are so entrenched that they are unconscious competencies. A "set" referral response program will usually have seven or eight procedures to adhere to that must be followed 100 percent of the time. An example of one of my referral procedures: at the bottom of every web page between my two websites—www.chuckbauer.com and www.cbsalestools.com—is a section asking for a referral, and this request is posted 24/7/365. It's working when I *sleep*. I learned about the superpower of a systematic referral system when I was selling for Nissan. For three consecutive years beginning in 1985, I did not accept one customer off the car lot because I was busy taking care of those that resulted from my referral system. And that *entire* program was conducted by mail. Nowadays, we have the Internet, e-mail (audio and

video), and other technologies. Last, be sure to use a referral response business card (described in detail in Chapter 5: Sales Tools.) Determine what kind of referral response program is best for you and *work it*! Engaging in this activity over and over will make clients chase you.

This is your chance to become a Sales S.T.U.D. No, not later; this offer will have expired tomorrow. Right *now* is your chance, so don't procrastinate and don't be lazy. Having and knowing your sales process reinforces your confidence. Enlighten prospects and clients to the consequences of living without your product or service. They don't even know what they're missing, so help to end that suffering by showing them the value that your product or service will add to their life today. Your urgency fosters *their* sense of urgency. Enhance their trust in you as well by authorizing a deadline for the transaction. You're either the leader or the follower in the sales-client relationship—which do you want to be?

Becoming a Sales S.T.U.D. Commission Development Quiz

Anything fewer than 100 percent correct answers requires immediate additional work!

1. What can you provide to the client that will cure his blurry vision of what's going to happen next in doing business with you? (Clue: It's the difference between wandering and dancing.)

2. What is the greatest client utilization tool known to man (when maximized)?

(continued)

(Continued)

3. Here is the definition; please provide the word that it describes: doing the thing you said you would do, long after the mood and emotion you said it in has left you.

4. This technique requires a prospect to do something to warrant their having the product, and only after the prospect has done their part does the salesperson give back the product. The name of this technique is also the same name given to the *really* good front-door parking spot at sit-down chain restaurants. The technique name fully embodies the principle of me thinking I was going to park there.

5. How many words are in the third paragraph of this chapter?

6. Aha! Now that you're at this point, this is your last chance to redeem yourself and prove you are coachable. If you really still haven't written this answer down, now answer: What are two takeaways that will work in your sales process?

7. You prevent delayed decisions by a customer when you create this.

8. What closes sales?

(continued)

(*Continued*)

9. What is the critical subject-line bait when going fishing via the Outlook calendar?

10. How many minutes would be realistically sufficient to illustrate the answer to number 9?

11. How many voicemails and e-mails is the limit to avoid the impression that you prefer to do the chasing?

12. Don't be _____.

13. Which of the 10 principles of a salesperson who is chased are you already doing?

14. Which of the 10 principles of a salesperson who is chased are you *not* already doing?

Becoming a Sales S.T.U.D. Quiz Answers

1. A specific next step

2. Outlook

3. Commitment

4. The takeaway

5. I'm just kidding

(*continued*)

(*Continued*)

6. Your answer

7. Urgency

8. Deadlines

9. "Quick"

10. Five minutes—which is demonstrated by manually changing the scheduled time in the drop-down menu in Outlook.

11. One of each contact method type. Be distinctive.

12. Lazy

13. Your answer

14. All of them

5

Bauer Power Sales Tools

Can you imagine a carpenter without a hammer? Or a surgeon without a scalpel? It doesn't work, does it? You've got to have tools for your craft, and you must be a specialist in using them. However, although they do exist, sales tools are—unfortunately—seldom used. If the majority of salespeople realized how much weight sales tools carry in buyer persuasion, they wouldn't allow themselves to go to work without them. A salesperson without sales tools at her disposal is making a major mistake. Once a salesperson understands this and develops a knowledgeable foundation about these tools, they should wear their tool belt with pride—knowing they're ready for *any* situation.

Know this: just "pitching the client" is a collision course—and when you crash, you'd better be prepared with your airbag of an apology. However, fully engaging your prospect will ease you through the sale on cruise control. Sales Tools allow you to fully engage the prospect and get them to actually *understand* your pitch! Involve your client completely with a visual (an image of your product or service), an explanation (either a third party testimonial or example of the product/service), and a concluding discussion (where *both* of you talk—not just you). Following these directions will set you on a positive course that will distinguish you from the competition.

Now the most rewarding point I can give you about using sales tools is this: **Sales Tools are *more* believable than you alone, just pitching.** Case in point: "I once caught a 33-pound catfish. But it didn't come easily. After the fish got stuck 100 feet offshore, I tore off all my clothes and went in, captured the fish with my bare hands, and brought it back to shore." Believable? No way. You automatically pawn it off as another fishing story. Your tendency to believe this story would—just like clients'—be at the lowest possible level. Then it proceeds to get worse as I, the story's "salesperson," keep talking: "Over the next five years, I caught the same fish two more times. And the last time I caught it, the fish weighed in at 49 pounds!" The more I talk, the more I discredit myself and impede the client's inclination to believe me.

Now watch what happens when I display my sales tools. "Here are photos of the fish taken at each of the three times I caught it. Here are also some magazine and newspapers articles verifying the catches, and last but not least, here is the State of Texas Record Certification of the fish. Oh—and here is the story in the words of my friend Jeff and his children, who witnessed the first catch." I have removed all doubt and uncertainty by the utilization of my sales tools; it now becomes irrefutable.

So get ready. It's time to find out how to catch the big fish and prove it's not just another fish story you're telling. Let's talk about bait, because big baits equal big fish—and big tools equal big sales.

Sales Tool #1: Your Website

When I'm addressing an audience about sales tools, I ask, "What is the one thing that a salesperson, corporate executive, or business owner should have before talking to clients? What is the first and most important sales tool?" Everyone invariably yells, "Business cards!" No way! There are many other options to be utilized in advance of any business card. Cards are not the first order of business. Establishing a domain name and setting up a personal website that promotes you, your product, and your company is absolutely paramount. Keep your website's name simple: companyname.com/yourname.com will do just fine. Furthermore, a one-to-two-page website is all that's necessary. Companies have been building increasingly elaborate websites for many years, it seems. Today, even major corporations are simplifying their websites, because people do not have or take the time to read pages of information.

However, having a simple website does not mean you can skimp on its development. I can't count the number of times I've had people say to me, "Oh, I think my second cousin has a friend who knows how to build websites." Absolutely not! You must work with a professional webmaster. Websites are one of the least expensive investments you'll ever make compared to the returns that it will offer. Your website is a reflection of *you*. Therefore, the highest level of professionalism is critical. Don't entrust something so important to your second cousin's best friend.

Of course, not all webmasters are created equal. You must find one who will build your website with successful marketing in mind. In this chapter, we continue to build on the ideas introduced in Chapter 3: Personality Selling, that in order to have the greatest impact your marketing pieces must appeal to both left-brain and right-brain personalities. Nowhere is this more important than on your website, which gives you turbo-charged marketing horsepower round-the-clock. A webmaster with a marketing-focused brain will know how to create a site that appeals to prospects' and clients' different personality preferences. Webmasters themselves naturally tend to be analytical engineering types—that is, thinkers. That doesn't mean, however, that every website they design should only attract like-minded people. Accountants' websites, for example, need more than just data and tax strategies if they are to entice socializers and relaters along with directors and thinkers. Likewise, your website needs to interest left-brain and right-brain personalities. If your webmaster is a thinker, you had better find someone with a marketing background to complement the webmaster. (See Figure 5.1.)

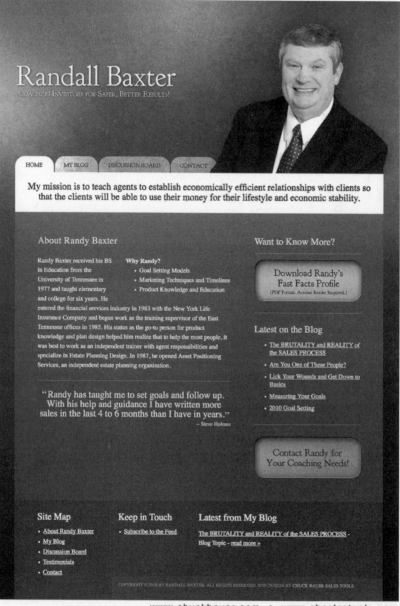

www.chuckbauer.com • www.cbsalestools.com

FIGURE 5.1

Sales Tool #2: A Fast Facts Profile (F.F.P.)

The next sales tool is a product called a Fast Facts Profile, or F.F.P. for short. The F.F.P is *by far* the best revenue-producer, F.U.D.-killer, and major intimacy-gaining device. This one simple tool has gained this power by having two very significant distinctions built into it. First, it is written professionally to speak to all four personality styles. (Have you heard that recently?) It does not matter if the prospect's preferred method of communication is ego-or feelings-based; the F.F.P will speak to either side of the brain, thus providing you with a solid selling advantage.

Secondly, the F.F.P. has multiple sales missiles. It is developed to have two photos—one, a formal headshot, and the other, a casual picture, either you with your family or exhibiting your passion (fishing, golf, travel, and so on)—appear alongside a professional as well as personal narrative about the salesperson, his or her company, and the products or services offered. My firm developed the F.F.P. in 1995 to help a major Dallas company improve client intimacy and closing-rate success. Business grew by *97 percent* over the course of one year, thanks to the F.F.P.'s ability to familiarize prospects with the company and make them feel more comfortable with the salespeople—*even before* a first appointment or call.

Back in 1995, some 90 percent of these profiles were faxed to clients; the remaining 10 percent was sent via e-mail. Today, there are thousands in circulation, with many also serving as one-page websites for salespeople.

Apart from providing an effective website, the profile has other important qualities and uses. An F.F.P is beneficial to give to clients before, during, or after a presentation; you can also ask clients to pass your profile along to referrals. Finally, make sure to print the F.F.P. on a sheet of high-quality, $8\frac{1}{2}$-by-11-inch paper stock from a professional printer, and *not* from the office copy machine. The Fast Facts Profile is a critical—and hopefully impressive—part of your staggered mail campaign, designed to increase the marks on a client's psychogenic scorecard. In all cases, the F.F.P. helps close more business—whether in the form of a website, e-mail, printed handout, or mailing. (See Figure 5.2.)

Powder Coat Your Products...

...with Georgia Powder Coating

Founded in 1999, Georgia Powder Coating has grown from 2 to over 30 employees in their own facility. Keeping customer service foremost in their core values, GPC has been regularly featured in "Powder Coating Tough," the industry's monthly magazine as a leader in the field.

About Georgia Powder Coating

We know that business presents you many challenges every day - including a fast paced, changing environment, parts needed yesterday and the necessity to ensure quality standards being consistently met.

At Georgia Powder Coating, our first priority is to simplify your life with a friendly environment, 3-day turnaround time, and intensive quality control measures. We have a proprietary process and systems designed to ensure that your parts are done right, on time, every time, making your life a little easier.

Why Dallas Cooley?

- A Nationally Recognized Powder Coating Expert
- Becomes a Client "Partner" on All Projects
- Knows That All Challenges Become Opportunities
- High Level of Experience with the Best Technology
- National Presence – Works Coast to Coast

About Dallas Cooley

Working directly with the owner of a company is unique in today's business world, yet this is exactly what you get when working with Dallas and Georgia Powder Coating. Dallas knows explicitly every process involved in your project, resulting in your success. Enthusiastic, energetic and committed to providing superior service to his clients, Dallas brings the commitment of personal ownership to every transaction with Georgia Powder Coating.

"Dallas & Georgia Powder Coating have always responded to our seemingly impossible requests for years with a willingness to get us what we need."

— Ricky Shirley
Lasercraft Technologies, Inc.

www.chuckbauer.com • www.cbsalestools.com

FIGURE 5.2

Are *You* Using *Distinctive* Sales Tools?

To answer this question, take a look at your business card. Does it list/show your company name and logo, your name and title, and your contact information? If so, I'm sorry to tell you that you're merely typical. There's nothing memorable there. This probably explains why your business card, like most, goes from a wallet to a wastebasket.

Of all the sales tools available, business cards are probably the most ubiquitous. So in order to be effective, a card must stand out from the masses. Take a look at my Main Point Card (M.P.C.), a unique sales tool that I developed. First of all, the card is *big*—3$\frac{1}{2}$ by 5 inches. In a stack of business cards, size matters. Second, it's two-sided and printed on heavy, high-gloss paper stock—because quality matters, too. Lastly, a quick reading of just one side lets prospects get to know me, my company, and the products and services that I sell, and how to contact me. Flip the card over and there is a partial client list and testimonials from satisfied clients. (See Figure 5.3.)

So whose business card is more distinctive and makes a better first impression? Yours or mine? Allow me to answer that question with a story. Jeff Crilley is a former Dallas TV news reporter who now heads a company called Real News Public Relations. My client, Trey Cure—president of Cure Financial—and I attended a seminar that Jeff was leading on marketing and public relations. Afterward, Trey and I stopped to talk with Jeff. Trey handed him his business card, and I gave him my Main Point Card.

Poor Trey; he was standing there with barely anything to say while Jeff and I discussed the size and marketing effectiveness of my M.P.C. When Trey returned to his office, he immediately e-mailed his insurance agents and told the story of me fostering a new client while he was "just taking up space," and ending the story with a directive to get rid of their old cards and order Main Point Cards pronto.

For those people who receive my M.P.C. and think, "This card is too big. It won't fit in my wallet," I answer, great! I've already begun building awareness of who I am, even if the card ends up in the trash. The rule of engagement here is that you need to penetrate

CHUCKBAUER

SALES CONSULTING
Sales Coaching & Consulting

SALES SEMINARS
Get Your Sales Force on Track

SALES MASTERMIND
Powerful Teleclasses

FREE VIDEOS & ARTICLES
Also Free SalesJava Classes

Contact Chuck Today!
www.chuckbauer.com
www.cbsalestools.com
(972) 740-4559

HIGH RESULTS
LOW COST
SALES TOOLS

GET YOURS TODAY!
www.cbsalestools.com

Partial Client List

New England Financial
CHASEHealthAdvance
Thomson Reuters
Capital Financial Services
Irwin Financial Group
CenterPoint Energy
Nissan / Verizon
Credit Answers
100's of Executive Sales Clients

"Chuck Bauer's SalesMastery course introduced new ideas and challenged existing mindsets while concentrating on sales. Though an outsider, Chuck's ownership mentality and commitment helped every sales person finish the training with an individualized goal and the enthusiasm to follow through, resulting in THREE back-to-back record sales weeks and TWO back-to-back RECORD SALES MONTHS!"

Scott Cato, Vice President of Sales, Credit Answers

"I increased my sales by 40% or a $203,000 annual gain & increased my income by over 35%!"

Matt West, SalesMastery Graduate

"Chuck's first two day session with my sales team increased our annual revenue by 50%. We have now rebooked him for four more additional seminars including his SalesMastery Course. His training seminars & ongoing accountability make all the difference!"

Bryon Thelen, Director of Sales, Thomson Reuters

"I've seen Chuck give many presentations. He's the essence of what a trainer, speaker, and motivator needs to be. I recommend you hire him today, before your competition does."

Jeffrey Gitomer

Go from ordinary to ... EXTRAORDINARY!

www.chuckbauer.com • www.cbsalestools.com

FIGURE 5.3

potential clients' brain blocks and become more deeply rooted in their awareness. Someone who says "That won't fit into my wallet" already gives me the upper hand in awareness compared to the same old boring, nondistinct business card.

And, by the way, I don't really care if the card is thrown away. In a few days, the person to whom I had given the card will receive another one as part of my staggered mail campaign. The point here is that I am building awareness. If you really cannot get past the notion of a larger card, then at least have a double-sided business card that offers clients more information. A single-sided card is completely nondistinct. I used to use those, too, back in the old days when I didn't know better. However, years of experience have taught me well; now you'll *never* find me carrying a single-sided card, let alone a card that is the same size as yours.

Sales Tools That Work for You

In addition to the Fast Facts Profile, there are several more sales tools to help you work smarter. Another results-fetching Sales Tools is the one-page sales sheet, which, like the F.F.P., has a variety of applications. It can be used in a face-to-face presentation, e-mailed as a low-resolution PDF during a live sales call, crumb-dropped as a leave-behind piece, included in your T.O.M.A. staggered mail campaign, loaded in a direct-marketing mail campaign, or served up as a simple one-page website. However you use it, the one-page sales sheets will give you powerful sales mileage. You make the sheet once and use it again and again. Here is a list of seven one-page sales sheet choices.

1. A **Standard Sales Pitch Sheet** (S.S.P.S.) is designed to back up your standard sales pitch, keeping it to three main points that the prospects will remember. A simple outline usually is sufficient here; it keeps the prospect on task with your presentation. You can include up to three corresponding benefits for each of main three significant points for a total of nine key statements. Include your contact information, logo, and branding—a rule that applies to all sales sheets. (See Figure 5.4.)

Standard Sales Pitch

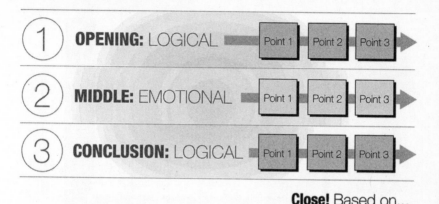

www.chuckbauer.com • www.cbsalestools.com

FIGURE 5.4

2. **The Overcoming Objection Sales Sheet** (O.O.S.S.) resists and eliminates client objections. There may be three or four ongoing objections that you encounter regularly within your industry. If you know that a certain protest is likely to be coming your way, an objection sheet allows you to refute a client's complaint in a prepared and professional manner. When you see the rain clouds moving in, grab your umbrella—just in case. These sheets can be mailed, e-mailed, or even loaded onto your website, much like the F.F.P. Have one sheet ready for each objection. Then, when your client mentions a specific doubt or concern, you have ammunition in the launch position, ready to kill the objection. Because it is from a third party source—the written and researched word—the sales sheet is *more* believable than you on your own, just spouting information. Use these in tandem with a trained Sales Mastery S.T.U.D.

    The number of objection sheets you need is irrelevant. Try to create one O.O.S.S. for as many objections you can anticipate. Figure 5.5 shows examples of two objection sheets used by our super-duper mortgage broker, Jeff Lang.

FIGURE 5.5

www.chuckbauer.com • www.cbsalestools.com

3. **A one-page Testimonial Sales Sheet (T.S.S.)** includes three or four client testimonials endorsing you, your company, and your product. You should also include your professionally designed logo and all of your contact information (Figure 5.6).

FIGURE 5.6

Consider establishing a **set policy or procedure** in an effort to gain testimonials from your clients. Based on experience, many of your clients may not want to write testimonials, either because they are too busy or feel that they lack writing skills. That's an easy protest to overcome; simply request that they provide you with some bullet points about their experience with you. Then hire a professional writer to compress their bullets points (clients always give too much information, even when you request "just a few" bullet points) and turn their information into a powerful and engaging two-to three-sentence testimonial. Have the client review and approve the finished product, then publish it on your one-page sales sheets, all marketing pieces, and your website. Obviously, if you are selling registered products and your company is regulated by FINRA, then you are forbidden by your compliance department to use testimonials. (See Figure 5.6.)

4. **Buyer's Remorse Prevention Package** (B.R.P.P.). This is what I refer to as a "burp" (just for fun). Many of you might be prone to cancellations from clients and prospects. Some might have to combat a three-day right of rescission, whereas others might experience an increase in cancelled appointments within the first four to six weeks of an enrollment of a new client. Regardless of the reasons (most of which usually relate to F.U.D.), a B.R.P.P. could prove useful in reminding clients *why* they enrolled in your program in the first place. It is designed to quell buyer's remorse and many of the other situations that may arise with your clients—such as the tendency for them to feel compelled to research a competitor for a better price the minute you disengage from them. Or when the office expert or urban advisor walks in after you leave and tells your client that they know of someone else in the same industry and can get them a better deal. In any event, create your B.R.P.P., put a **set policy** in place, and implement this tool immediately. Helpful hint: one of my sales students, who is a master of in-home sales, keeps numerous B.R.P.P.s in a box in his car. After each closing, he personally addresses an envelope containing one of these pages and drops it off at the closest post office. Now *that's* fast follow-up.

5. **Promise Makers/Promise Keepers Sales Sheet** (P.M.S.S.) Another client of mine, Electronic Sales Company in Gainesville, Georgia, has a small sales staff. The sales side of their company is known as the Promise Makers, while the service side of their business is called the Promise Keepers. I suggested to them to turn those "promises" into a page, which is now a useful multipurpose sales sheet. On the left column of the sheet, we indicate the promises "made" by the Promise Makers. On the right column of the sheet, we indicate the promises "kept" by the Promise Keepers. This is a quick and simple way for clients to see not only what you're doing for them, but that you've indeed kept your word about all those claims that you made back in the beginning of the sales process.

6. **Referral Response Sales Sheet** (R.R.S.S.). This tool provides another way to ask for referrals from clients. Again, you must penetrate a client's awareness many times before they freely give up a referral—and the R.R.S.S. does just that. It offers the recipient the ability to fill out a form with the critical information and data on multiple referrals. The form should display your logo, branding, contact information, and a brief description of how you will treat your referral. This type of page also has the potential to become an online referral form.

7. **Special Event Sales Sheet** (S.E.S.S.). This is a single page for promoting and disseminating information about upcoming special events. I lead many different seminars in and around the Dallas–Fort Worth Metroplex, and my Creative Services Team always uses the same S.E.S.S. It only takes a few seconds to change the data, and presto—we are off to the races with a template form that can be used over and over without having to duplicate our efforts, or needing to recreate this document.

Remember this: one-page sales sheets have many uses and functions when utilized at the highest levels of sales efficiency. Each one should be professionally printed on high-quality paper stock and used for presentations, website resources leave-behinds, enclosures in a staggered mail campaign, and via e-mail as a low resolution, fast-load document. One sales sheet equals multiple missiles. Simply launch them, and watch them hit your targets.

The next Power Sales Tool that you should have in your arsenal is a **Referral Response Card (R.R.C.),** which should always be cocked and loaded into your referral program and your T.O.M.A. campaign. Like the Main Point Card, the R.R.C. is $3\frac{1}{2}$ by 5 inches and double-sided. There is typically a graphic to indicate that you are hunting for referrals. If you are after a certain type of referral, then ask for it. Use this tool just as the others—along with the Jim Rohn book, staggered mailings, and e-mailed as a low-resolution fast-loading PDF. (See Figure 5.7.)

Another avenue for referrals is your website. We have a request for referrals at the bottom of every page on my two websites. As a result, we obtain five to seven referrals every week. We're not pounding on clients' doors, but asking is a vital part of our referral program. Whenever I question an audience about the last time they asked for a referral, someone typically responds, "Oh, about a week ago." A referral program with set policies and procedures is a *must* for every salesperson in any sales organization.

For clients with whom communication has been lacking, well, it may be time to send them a pink slip. No, not *that* kind of pink slip; I mean the one that is often used for writing down telephone messages. I must give credit where credit is due: this terrific idea came from Chris Galambos, a student of mine who works for CenterPoint Energy in East Texas. There are three free templates that can be downloaded from my website at www.chuckbauer.com/pink and used for follow-up with prospects or clients you haven't heard from lately. One is a PDF file, which looks like the pink phone message slip that was so useful before voicemail. Simply fill in the blanks and send it in PDF form. Next is another PDF that prints in black and white, allowing you to fax or mail copies to clients. The third is an html version that is small enough to copy and paste into the body of an e-mail.

FIGURE 5.7

These pink slips are great for producing "sales time." The one I send by e-mail most frequently is not dated or time-stamped, and doesn't specifically name any particular client. Instead, I send each one to "VIP Client" with a date of "Today" and the time as "Now"—an approach that allows me to send the same pink slip via e-mail hundreds of times without ever changing a thing! None of the information changes for a standard message, making this a great way to touch clients, save time, and drive up revenue. Prospects and clients get a kick out of these pink slips because they are unique and have a retro look, and often tell me so. In fact, a few of my e-mailed pink slips have actually induced client callbacks wherein the person on the other hand apologized for missing my call, but let me know that they received the pink slip and were touching base with me. H-e-l-l-o! I *never* called them; all I did was send the pink slip via e-mail. Talk about creating *top of mind awareness*! (See Figure 5.8.)

Similarly, professionally created e-mail signatures create a positive impression and increase the chances that clients will instantly recognize you. Your e-mail signature should be in a low-resolution format and include your name and photo, your company name, and your website, e-mail address, and phone number. A custom e-mail signature graphic will provoke interest, a business boost, or a sense of intrigue to your e-mail communications. It can be altered based on time of year or holiday greetings; you can have a new graphic every month or once a quarter and have them hyperlinked to your website. (See Figure 5.9.)

That e-mail signature will come in handy as you send video and audio e-mails. Why should your clients receive ho-hum, *yawn*, typed messages when a distinctive salesperson like yourself can send a full-color *talking* message? The e-mail video craze is only beginning to take off; start sending video e-mails today, and you can stay ahead of the sales pack. Of course, if this is a bad hair day or if you don't particularly like your outfit, then an audio e-mail works well, too. When clients open either the video or audio, your graphic is alongside the e-mail display screen. Clicking on that graphic takes clients directly to your website. There are many inexpensive video and audio programs available; you can easily find them by searching

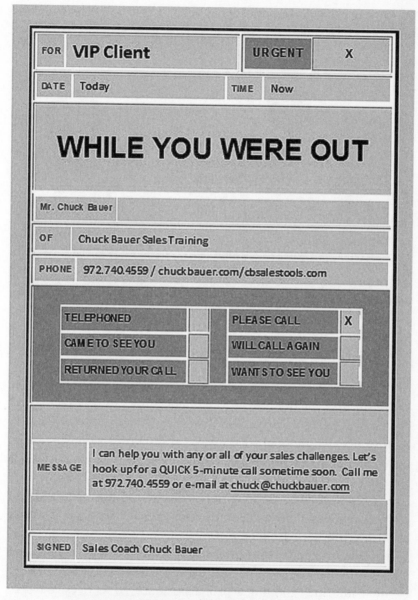

FOR **VIP Client** URGENT X

DATE Today TIME Now

WHILE YOU WERE OUT

Mr. Chuck Bauer

OF Chuck Bauer Sales Training

PHONE 972.740.4559 / chuckbauer.com/cbsalestools.com

TELEPHONED		PLEASE CALL	X
CAME TO SEE YOU		WILL CALL AGAIN	
RETURNED YOUR CALL		WANTS TO SEE YOU	

MESSAGE I can help you with any or all of your sales challenges. Let's hook up for a QUICK 5-minute call sometime soon. Call me at 972.740.4559 or e-mail at chuck@chuckbauer.com

SIGNED Sales Coach Chuck Bauer

Pink Slip 'Em is freely distributed by Sales Coach Chuck Bauer.
Visit www.chuckbauer.com/pink or www.cbsalestools.com for more information.

www.chuckbauer.com • www.cbsalestools.com

FIGURE 5.8

the Internet or checking the Resources section at the back of this book. Most basic packages start at $40 per month.

FIGURE 5.9

Social *sales* media sites, such as Facebook, YouTube, Plaxo, LinkedIn, and Twitter, offer more opportunities to reach prospects and clients online. However, we salespeople need to use these sites to drive *revenue*—not our social lives. Far too many people use social media to chitchat with friends; we use social *sales* media to sell our products and services.

These sites offer unique opportunities to brand yourself and consistently keep your name in front of clients. Facebook, Twitter, and LinkedIn are excellent platforms from which to adapt social *sales* media branding—you can capture referrals, testimonials, and important questions from clients. They are also a great way to keep clientele informed about new products, improved services, and special events. Moreover, your social sales media page will not get lost in a haze of junk e-mails or, worse, deleted!

Be sure to brand your page with your logo, colors, and identifying elements; this is an important persuasive marketing strategy to help set your company apart from your competitors. Make your mark. Doing so will give your clients that all-important top of mind awareness (T.O.M.A.) that causes them to think of you first.

My rule for brochures and other general marketing materials is that *less is more*. In other words, make the text concise rather than verbose. This is a brochure, not a legal document written by an attorney. Use bullet points, laser-focused phrases, and bolded fonts to emphasize important points and break the uniformity of the text. Moreover, use only graphics that are of the highest quality, and keep the layout precise. Don't make the mistake of taking short cuts to save money. What you end up truly cutting back on is the professionalism of your business impression. You may as well give your next presentation on construction paper with glitter and glue, and pitch it while selling ten-cent lemonade for backup. If you want to attract and impress prospects and clients, then spend the extra money to have your marketing materials professionally written and designed.

Of course, we can't forget Jim Rohn's *Excerpts from the Treasury of Quotes*, an outstanding sales tool for winning respect from clients that distinguishes you and your company and takes advantage of the law of reciprocation. If you're a salesperson who sells to salespeople, send the *Sales Mastery Book of Quotes* by Chuck Bauer.

Now that you've spun the racks of a few best results-getters, no matter which sales tools you decide to use, remember: *outta sight, outta mind—in sight, in mind*.

I can recall one particular day when I was in Florida doing a sales tune-up for one of my client companies. I came onto their sales floor knowing full well that all the salespeople had their Main Point Cards printed about 30 days earlier, and was fully expecting to hear some great stories of client awareness from using their Main Point Cards.

Great stories? None. Laziness? Full out. Why no success stories? Every stack of 500 cards was *still* tightly enclosed in its cellophane wrapper. This absolutely sent me through the roof! I was beyond disappointed. That sales department heard about it—and you will, too. So, salespeople, listen up! Your sales tools attract no more sales activity than does your paper clip jar when sitting in an office cupboard or desk drawer. If your professionally created sales tools have ink that is pale from antiquity, or if they've gathered enough dust to finger-write "wash me" on them, then you need to check yourself. Sales tools, like Delta Airline jet airplanes, make money only when they "are in the air!"

On a subsequent trip about eight months later, the sales department at this particular company requested that I do a chair-side training session with a rookie named Fred. Fred was all excited about having the Sales Coach work with him on live calls. At the end of his first significant sales call, I asked Fred where his Main Point Cards were. Guess what? Uh-huh. The cards were ash-white from sitting around *and* they were still in the cellophane wrapper. I looked down on Fred's desk and there was a beautiful family photo of Fred's son, Fredrick II, who was really cute. He had a great smile, and appeared to be about three years old.

So I made a deal with Fred. Anytime that any salesperson, manager, or the Sales Coach found Fred's desk void of his Main Point Cards and envelopes, Fred would be asked to place Fredrick II's photo in the cave (drawer). Fredrick II would have to stay in the cave until such time that Fred's Main Point Cards and envelopes reappeared. It seemed very simple to me. If we need to establish a college education fund for Fredrick II through an increase in sales, then the sales tools would have to be fully engaged 100 percent of the time. "Become fully engaged or become completely disengaged!" Fred got the hint. (See Figure 5.10.)

Of course, if you have an established T.O.M.A. campaign as discussed in the Marketing Yourself Shamelessly chapter, it may just save you from blunders like these.

Having the right sales tools helps you to start and end the job properly and efficiently. But don't store them in a drawer or someplace else where you cannot see them; like other tools, they won't work if they're hidden away. Instead, keep your sales tools visible and close at hand to remind yourself to use them. And always make sure that your logo and other graphics—as well as photographs and other branding—are done professionally from the start. Do not settle for hijacking low-resolution photographs off the Internet.

Outta Sight Outta Mind   **In Sight** In Mind

www.chuckbauer.com • www.cbsalestools.com

FIGURE 5.10

Whether you are a salesperson, sales manager, business owner, or corporate executive, positive first impressions are vital; you only have one shot at making them. A professional should *never* be without the proper tools. Perhaps even more important, he or she is only proved to be a professional through disciplined *use* of those tools. The carpenter that hasn't used his hammer or the surgeon who last used his scalpel during the last lunar eclipse is likely to be unemployed.

**Bauer Power Sales Tools Commission
Development Quiz**

Anything fewer than 100 percent correct answers requires immediate additional work!

1. _____ (two words) allow you to fully engage the prospect and helps them understand your pitch.

(continued)

(*Continued*)

2. If your business card is not your most important sales tool, then what is?

3. Which sales tool speaks to all four personality styles in an $8^1/_2$-by-11-inch well-designed package?

4. True or False: The tools named in question #3 *also serve as salespeople's one-page websites.*

5. Is it okay if a prospect throws your business card into the trash?

6. A _____ with set policies and procedures is a must for every salesperson in any sales organization.

7. A S_____ S_____ P_____ Sheet is designed to back up your standard sales pitch, keeping it down to three main points that the prospects will remember.

8. The O_____ O_____ S_____ S_____ combats and eliminates objections.

9. A one-page T_____ S_____ S_____ includes three or four client

(*continued*)

(*Continued*)

testimonials endorsing you, your company, and your product.

10. A B_____ R_____
    P_____ P_____ is
    designed to kill buyer's remorse and many of the other situations that may arise with your clients.

11. Besides using your mouth, the other way to ask for referrals is to utilize a R_____
    R_____ Sales Sheet.

12. Since it takes several penetrations into the client's awareness before a referral is given up, what are two other methods for requesting a referral?

13. What are the two advancements beyond typing yet another ho-hum e-mail to a client?

14. Taking shortcuts and cost cuts on your marketing and sales materials actually shortcuts what?

15. For an obvious and immediate distinction, for what tool do you need to immediately swap your blandy-dandy business card?

16. Once you have the tools, what do you do with them?

(*continued*)

(*Continued*)

Bauer Power Sales Tools Quiz Answers

1. Sales tools

2. Domain name and personal website

3. Fast Facts Profile

4. True

5. Yes, so long as it was distinctive.

6. Referral program

7. Standard Sales Pitch Sheet (S.S.P.S.)

8. Overcoming Objection Sales Sheet

9. Testimonial Sales Sheet

10. Buyer's Remorse Prevention Package

11. Referral Response

12. Referral Response Card and website request

13. Video-and audio-messaging

14. Your professionalism and business impression

15. Main Point Card

16. Use them!

6

Communication Mastery

Wake up, check e-mail. Make coffee, check text messages. Get dressed, listen to voice messages. Eat breakfast, call sales manager. Start car, text first client. Arrive at office, check e-mail again.

Although this scenario may not apply to you in every respect, it does demonstrate just how much communication we salespeople can have in only a few hours. Experts estimate that we spend more than 80 percent of our day communicating—and if we know how to maximize advances in wireless technology, the Internet, and automated transmissions, we can even have meaningful communication while we're sleeping! No wonder those outdated selling systems that used guerrilla tactics no longer work. Today, salespeople must regard every person they meet as a potentially lifelong relationship. Therefore, mastering communication skills is critical for growing a salesperson's business.

Humans typically communicate at a 30 percent efficiency rate. That means that 7 out of 10 messages are misunderstood, mistaken, missed, or just plain messed up in one way or another. And regarding salespeople and business owners, that rate falls off significantly. Do you know that many of you begin your sales phone calls with "Hey!" Or how about this frequent communication violator: "How you doing great!" This salesperson just blasted through a discussion and went as far as having a discussion with himself in a matter of seconds while totally destroying his ability to really get connected with the prospect. This is how it should have gone: "*How* are you doing?" [pause] "I am doing fine, thanks for asking." [pause] "How are you?" [pause] "I'm *great.*"

Consider the sales that might have been lost because of such miscommunication. Just imagine what a 50, 60, or even 80 percent communication efficiency rate would do for your revenue potential. So let's move you from your current AM frequency and get you some Sirius satellite radio.

Mastering communication requires some tips that are specifically important for salespeople and business owners.

1. **Be enthusiastic.** In any communication with clients, enthusiasm outsells product knowledge. Having coached hundreds of salespeople on phone sales and in one-on-one meetings, I can attest to the fact that animation, passion, gusto—call it whatever you like—clinches the deal more so than spouting details about the product or service. I've worked with salespeople who are hesitant to make a call until they fully understand every last detail of a product or service. But you know what? That doesn't matter as much as showing that you're passionate about what you are selling. So put some enthusiasm in your voice and make that phone call. I once had a company vice president send me 27 MP3 files of recorded phone conversations between her salespeople and prospects. I went through the first couple minutes of about ten calls before I realized the problem was a complete lack of animation in their expression. Every salesperson's voice was a monotonous song of Morse code; it sounded just like someone reading from a script. Remember what we discussed before: *ignorance on fire will always outsell knowledge on ice.*

2. **Be accurate and precise.** Although you must strive to communicate with clients according to their dominant personality styles, the facts and claims you present in your message must always be accurate. In other words—say what you mean and mean what you say. Precision relates to your appointment times. If you are early, you're a salesperson, if you're on time, you're a genius, and if you're late, you're a bozo. At least, that's what your clients think.

3. **Be authentic.** Along with great enthusiasm, communication needs some authentic emotion. Speak from your heart. Be sincere. Otherwise you're a plastic pink flamingo—and prospects and clients can spot a fake in a heartbeat.

4. **Don't be adrenalized.** There's a difference between enthusiasm and exaggeration. Don't overinflate the value of your product or service. Unnecessary claims and false guarantees will only get you in trouble.

5. **Don't stretch the truth.** At the end of a month, salespeople tend to resort to fabrication, exaggeration, or data omission in a last-ditch effort to reach their quota. High-level salespeople who have taken the time to hone their skills usually reach their sales goals by the 20th or 21st of the month. They don't stoop to lying, cheating, or miscommunicating with clients in order to close sales, and neither should you. Instead of being a *defective* elaborator, learn to be an *effective* communicator.

The following communication practices—though not specific to sales situations—are generally helpful in delivering your message.

1. **Make eye contact**. If you are speaking to more than one person, hold eye contact for at least three seconds and then connect with another person. If you are engaged in phone sales, use a mirror and connect up by observing your facial expressions, and *smile*!

2. **Use positive speech connectors**, such as "Yes," "Great," "Wonderful," "Keep it going," and "Tell me more." These and similar types of words keep people in the conversation loop.

3. **Tune in to the meaning** behind someone's words. That is, read between the lines. If Sherry the client says, "Buying that car might be a good idea," Jack the salesperson should hear, "I'm drawn to the product, but I need more information to make a decision."

4. Train yourself to **speak no more than 140 to 160 words per minute**, the speed at which the human brain can best process dialogue. This will be discussed further in the next chapter, Presentation Mastery.

5. Make sure your **body language** is in agreement with your words and your tone. For example, if you are enthused, then convey this excitement through your smile, voice, and posture.

6. **Don't overreact** when provoked. Always underrespond. If the client states "I don't like you!" You respond calmly with "Okay, now that we have that out of the way, allow me to show you this feature. . . ."

7. Focus on the **personality differences** among people and adapt to them when conversing. Remember, the four basic personality styles all want to receive communication in their own style, not yours.

8. **Eliminate titles**, such as Mr., Mrs., or Ms., and address people by their first names.

9. **Take notes** during your meetings. It not only demonstrates that you deeply value the client's feedback and aren't giving them the chance to forget any details, it also plants the seeds for follow-up communication. A more efficient method would be to take notes on your laptop, BlackBerry, and/or iPad (and make sure to tell the prospect that you are taking notes, lest they assume that you're e-mailing your Facebook buddies!)

10. **Be consistently visible** with your prospects and clients by way of an active T.O.M.A. campaign. This continues the relationship with the client. Consider it fan mail for your customer.

Do You Want to Know A Secret? Listen, I'll Tell You

www.chuckbauer.com • www.cbsalestools.com

FIGURE 6.1

And there you have it—that's the secret. *Listening*—the communication skill that outweighs all others. (See Figure 6.1.) Apart from the need for food, shelter, and love, humans need to be heard. An effective communicator has mastered listening. The ability of a salesperson to *truly listen* to prospects and clients gives you a distinction over your competitors who are soothed by the penniless sounds of their own voices.

Picture a salesperson and a client having a conversation, either in person or over the phone. The client begins what I call a language thread: their statement and/or question tied to the total number of words. In this example, let's say that the prospect's thread comprises 100 words. After how many words do you think the salesperson stops listening? Ten? Twenty-five? Seventy? Or all 100? What do you think? Most people in the audiences I teach guess the answer is between 30 to 50 words. Sadly, this is wishful thinking; the correct answer is *seven*. Most salespeople stop listening after only *seven words*. (See Figure 6.2.)

Master Intimacy—Master the Connection

➡ **100** ➡
WORDS

THE CLIENT

SALES-PERSON

When the "need" to be _____ is fulfilled, _____ is gained when we move closer to _____.

www.chuckbauer.com • www.cbsalestools.com

FIGURE 6.2

But wait. The situation gets *worse*. Between the seventh and the tenth word, a salesperson quickly formulates a response to what is being said. The client has barely begun speaking—and the salesperson is ready to reply! As if that weren't bad enough, somewhere between the 11th and 100th words, a salesperson will either interrupt or simply stop paying attention to what the client says.

If you have a habit of interrupting, try to stop. At least put on the brakes before you crash your client's respect for you. On the other hand, you might find yourself occasionally glancing at your watch, drumming your fingers on the desk, or folding your arms and tapping your toe as you wait for a client to stop talking. Think of what you might learn if you tuned in! I have students ask me, "Chuck, why can't I close these people?" The answer is likely in the clues the client offers somewhere between words number 11 and 100. However, if you're not listening or if you've interrupted, then you're obviously not going to hear those clues. Become a master listener. Embrace what a client says and you'll be able to use that information to close a sale.

Now that we know how much we can gain by not interrupting clients and listening attentively to what they say, let's go a step further. When clients have finished speaking . . . shhh! Be quiet for a few seconds, and remember P.S.P.—pause, silence, patience. A P.S.P. moment creates a brief gap in conversation and gives your clients what I call the Psychogenic Green Light to continue speaking. This in turn signals that *you* have a green light to continue listening for important clues to help you in closing. If they want to mention something else, this gap lets them know they may continue—and that you are respectfully listening. Clients appreciate such consideration, because most salespeople are too busy pitching to pause.

When clients know they are being heard, then your relationships with them move beyond rapport toward intimacy. As the House of Connectability (see Figure 3.1) demonstrates, intimacy with clients provides a level of comfort that eliminates the fear, uncertainty, and doubt, or F.U.D. As a result, you will be able to close more deals. Know this: F.U.D. festers in the kiss-up, suck-up, and rapport-building stages. Blast the F.U.D. outta-sight by gaining a high level of intimacy with your prospects and clients.

Words and Phrases That Foster Intimacy

● Appreciate ● Respect ● Agree ● Okay ● May I comment?
● Recommend ● Because ● Yes ● And ● Honor ● Challenge
● I'm sorry ● My apologies ● Grateful

Words and Phrases That Shatter Intimacy

● Hey ● Hey, you ● Can't ● Possibly ● Hope ● Try ● Maybe
● Yeah ● Yeah, but ● But ● Whatever ● Problem ● Um
● I dunno ● If ● I'm busy ● Just ● Basically

Questions and Statements That Help Build Intimacy

- Tell me about you.
- Tell me about your business.
- What do you think about . . . ?
- What would you suggest . . . ?
- What will you accomplish by . . . ?
- What would happen if . . . ?
- What do you think is a better way?
- What's your biggest concern?
- How important is that to you?
- Why is it being done that way?
- Can you give me an example of . . . ?
- What do you like most about . . . ?
- What do you find is effective?

To determine whether you are listening well enough to achieve intimacy with your clients, consider the following eight questions. Answer N for not applicable or none, and assign 0 point for this answer, B for beginner, and assign 1 point for this answer, I for intermediate, and assign 2 points for this answer, and A for advanced, and assign 3 points for this answer. The total possible score is 24 points.

1. Do you simultaneously and conscientiously process a **client's tone of voice** as well as the words being spoken? If you said "I'm happy" in a grumbling growl, I'd think you were sarcastic and possibly quite aggravated or angry, despite your words. It would certainly have a different meaning if you said it in a sing-song, Julie Andrews voice, in which case I'd assume that you were elated and extremely pleased. Tone of voice will sometimes tell more than words themselves.

2. Do you hear **what is not being said**? This is strongly connected with your level of intimacy with the client. Did your client seem to hesitate before he answered your question? You may have just missed a hint that they are still seeking reasons to trust you, your product or service, or your company. It is usually a challenge for directors and thinkers to tune into this, because the intuition required to detect nonspoken messages is mainly a feelings-based skill. Though directors and thinkers *can* of course do this, it takes practice and years of experience to cultivate this pearl of a skill.

3. Do you completely hear and understand your prospects' **needs and challenges**? Can you relate to and identify with them?

4. Do you recognize clients' **understatements, overstatements, or misrepresentations**? In other words, can you detect when *they're* feeding *you* a line?

5. Are you **listening** or are you getting ready to respond?

6. **Do you insert gaps** as you converse with clients—10, 15, or 20 seconds of silence during which clients can interject another thought?

7. Do you **recognize the critical needs** of your prospects and clients by listening to them?

8. Do you merely hear what a client says or **do you listen *for* the client's message** and look for feedback? Not listening is not hearing anything, "listening to" is when you hear what they're saying with passive acknowledgment ("Uh-huh," "Sure," and so on), and "listening for" is total conversational engagement.

If your scored above 20 points, congratulations! If you scored below 20, you need to pay attention to the training in this chapter.

Now that you've assessed your listening skills, what do you think are some things you can do to become a better listener? First of all, follow **Bauer's Rule of One Thousand**, which states that for every 1,000 words a client speaks, a salesperson should speak 100. Most salespeople unfortunately reverse this rule, however. A client may only manage to eke out 10 words as the salesperson rambles on and on. I have sat in on more than my share of live sales presentations during which the salesperson spoke 1,000 to 5,000 words without even coming up for air! As he turned blue in the face, the salesperson needed a breathing tube stuck up his nose to ensure the flow of oxygen. But, nah; I wanted to watch him pass out. The old maxim is true: there's a reason why God gave humans two ears and one mouth—**so we would listen twice as much as we speak**. Remember that.

The next tactic you can use to become a better listener is the top-secret question previously discussed in the chapter on Personality Selling. After opening the conversation with a bit of small talk, simply say: "Tell me about you." Then *be quiet and listen to the response*. You are likely to glean information about the prospect's personality style within the first ten words out of their mouth. And if you happen to be asked a question during your conversation, stop and think, "Can I answer that with one word?" If yes, reply with one word—and then continue to listen. The challenge here is to not follow that one word with one other specific word that causes self-destruction—but. "Yes, and...," "No, but...," "Okay, well...," After that, Bauer's Rule is almost certain to be broken.

The conjoined twin to the important listening tactic of not interrupting is *concentrating*. When clients speak, do you really concentrate on what they are telling you, or are you distracted by your computer, a text message, or something else? I realize that sometimes your job necessitates logging data as you are having a conversation. But once that task is completed, turn away from the computer or your cell phone and continue to focus on the conversation. The needle of the focus-meter measuring your level of concentration takes a quick spin downward faster than a Hollywood star dropping out of rehab when you have distractions like a cell phone call, text message, or an e-mail. I'm fully aware that some salespeople practically live and breathe by their phone. But you know what? You sucker *yourself* into phone slavery. There is a simple solution, however, to staying focused: *turn off your cell phone ringer*. Personally, I answer my phone at my own convenience, not anyone else's. This allows me to keep my focus meter at the highest possible level during all client communications, not to mention maintaining my ability to concentrate for the entire sales day.

Last but not least—please be patient. Patience will go a long way in earning your client's respect and trust. Don't forget, you are setting a precedent for a lifelong relationship with prospects and clients, because they are directly affecting your income and lifestyle. Show them you're worthy of that relationship by doing what's responsible. You must *earn* the right to engage in that lifelong connection.

Characteristics of Great Listeners versus Poor Listeners

Great Listeners. . . .

- **Make eye contact.** Did you know that you can do this even over the phone? Place a mirror alongside your computer to know whether or not you are smiling during conversations with clients. Trust me—other people can "hear" your smile. The eyes are the window to our soul.

(continued)

(*Continued*)

- Ask **open-ended questions**. These types of questions require discussion, such as "Tell me about your specific needs and challenges . . . ?"

- **Concentrate and acknowledge** what a client says with comments such as "Thank you; I appreciate that," "I understand," or "I honor what you just said."

- Remain **poised and emotionally in control**. Even if a client says, "I don't like you, I don't like your company, I don't like your product, I don't like the state that you live in, and I don't like your first name," your response must be cool and understated: "Okay, great." Then move on to the next step in your presentation. Many people just want to test you, especially those who are directors. So don't lose your temper.

Poor Listeners . . .

- Are distracted and frequently change the subject.
- Interrupt, jump to conclusions, and finish clients' sentences for them.
- Are impatient and fidget.
- Overreact and lose their tempers.
- Often are caught saying this: "Yeah, yeah, yeah, yeah, yeah . . ."
- Speak too quickly, at a rate of about 180 to 220 words per minute. (As previously mentioned, no more than 140 to 160 words per minute is optimal.)

Personality Styles and Communication

As we've established, one's preferred method of communication is closely linked to one's personality style. And just as there are four personalities types—directors, socializers, relaters, and thinkers—there are four forms of communication:

1. A novel.
2. A short story.
3. Laser-focused phrases.
4. Bullet points.

Can you match the personality style to the communication style?

Regardless of a salesperson's dominant personality style, each of us begins communication with a concept that we want to convey to our prospect or client and a desired end result. In between is the time required to relay our message. Thinkers tend to need the most time, since they communicate in novels. Socializers prefer short stories, relaters use laser-focused phrases, and directors speak in bullet points.

Does being a socializer mean that you cannot communicate like a director? Of course not. For example, I frequently have corporate clients who want me to give identical presentations to a large group of people and then to the board of directors. The challenge is that I have an hour for the large group, but only 10 minutes for the board. Thus I formulate the concept and the end result, and then adjust the time frame in between. The hour-long presentation is compressed in order to deliver the same concept in 10 minutes; the short story becomes a list of bullet points, but I am able to convey the same general concept.

Regardless of the form of communication, the important point here is that it's what the clients remember that counts. Can anyone recollect everything spoken in a one-hour sales presentation or 5,000 to 50,000 words from a speech? Not unless you're the Rain Man. In a typical sales situation, your prospect or client will remember only three main points. Consequently, shorter is best: try to use laser-focused phrases and bullet points even if you are inclined to speak in novels and short stories. If you don't believe in the "less is more" approach, then answer this question: what was President Lincoln's most famous speech ever delivered? The Gettysburg

Address. At only three paragraphs long, *this golden presentation utilized only 268 words.* No novels, no short stories—just laser-focused phrases and bullet points. That speech is immortalized in the history of our nation.

Indeed, throughout the course of history, bullet points or laser-focused phrases have proved to play a very significant part of what is remembered about a particular speech or event. Consider the following quotes.

> The only thing we have to fear is fear itself.
> *—President Franklin Roosevelt* **in his Great Depression speech**

> I have nothing to offer but blood, toil, tears, and sweat.
> *—Prime Minister Winston Churchill* **at the beginning of World War II**

> Ask not what your country can do for you; ask what you can do for your country.
> *—President John Kennedy* **in his 1961 inaugural speech**

> That's one small step for man, one giant leap for mankind.
> *—Astronaut Neil Armstrong,* **the first person to walk on the moon**

> Mr. Gorbachev, tear down this wall!
> *—President Ronald Reagan* **at Brandenburg Gate in West Berlin**

> Don't overthink the think; *overdo* the *do*!
> *—Sales Coach Chuck Bauer* **instructing sales students**

In communication and listening, the four personality styles demonstrate areas of strength and areas for development. Let's look at each in detail.

Among directors' strengths are the ability to get to the point, offer clear feedback, concentrate on a task, help others focus, encourage organization, and identify inconsistencies in communication. However, they can be impatient with people who ramble, and are likely to jump to conclusions before a conversation has ended. They are also easily distracted if they become bored. Directors will sometimes minimize socializers' or relaters' feelings or be overly critical when communicating with them. They are usually unaware of this behavior.

Socializers' strong suit is that they are expressive, optimistic, engaging, and naturally enthusiastic. They are the ones who attempt to include everyone in the conversation in large groups. Because they are easygoing, socializers prefer informality, a preference that usually benefits them. Socializers are also more flexible with their time, which is an advantage when they are interacting with other socializers. However, socializers would be wise to watch the clock in sales situations with directors or thinkers.

Like directors, socializers can be impatient. They may talk over clients, saying "Yeah, yeah, yeah" because they want them to hurry up and finish, so that they can continue chatting. Similarly, socializers are the most likely of all salespeople to interrupt. And because they are so creative and emotional—very right-brained—they sometimes lose concentration when communicating.

Although there aren't many of them in the sales world, relaters make the best listeners. They are caring, concerned, and nonjudgmental, and can easily identify with people's varying moods and emotions. On the downside, relaters may become entangled with their feelings and unnecessarily internalize concerns. As a result, they may miss out on a sale if the prospect is ready to buy, yet the relater is unsure of the product or service—and unknowingly conveys this uncertainty to the prospect. Relaters often have trouble recognizing clients' negative characteristics, and are easily pushed to the side by more dominant personalities. They will not call clients out on their self-induced bullsh—t.

Thinkers' strong points are that they encourage support, they value data received through communication and welcome complex information, and analyze that information, as well as all communications between themselves and a specific client. On the other side of the coin, thinkers' gifts for acquiring knowledge and information can become detrimental if they fixate *too* intensely on details when speaking with socializers, relaters, or directors. Moreover, their intelligence can be intimidating. They may minimize the value of information not proved by data, and will frequently discredit nonexperts. Also, like thinker clients who require a good deal of time before deciding whether to purchase, thinker salespeople prefer a long decision-making process—and will occasionally even talk themselves *out* of a sale. While a prospect may say, "I'm ready to buy now—here is the cash for the order!" the thinker salesperson replies with, "But wait, there's more I have to tell you!"

Circle of Communication

Whether you are a director, socializer, relater, or thinker, nearly all salespeople are *complainers* at one time or another. This is not too surprising; people in general like to complain, grumble, whine, bellyache, moan, and gripe. However, complaining is a low-level and ineffectual communication tactic that needs to be replaced. But with what?

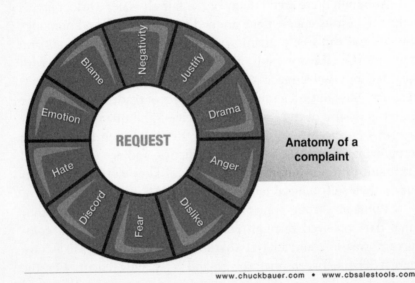

FIGURE 6.3 Circle of Communication

Let's consider the Circle of Communication depicted in Figure 6.3. The outer ring consists of the elements of a complaint: negativity, justification, drama, anger, dislike, fear, discord, hate, emotion, and blame. At the core of a complaint, however, is a request. Thus, instead of registering a complaint, salespeople should remove all the other parts of the statement and simply say, "I have a request." Follow that with the details of what you need.

I know sales managers across the country who, when a salesperson comes to them with a complaint, will redirect that person to return when they are ready to make a request. In fact, some managers actually *fine* salespeople who complain. Over time, salespeople learn to stop complaining and start requesting, since this is a much more powerful communication tactic. Complaining displays sales immaturity and, more often than not, turns you into what I call a "project." I always advise the sales managers with whom I work to *avoid projects*. Don't hire them and don't keep them. They're very disruptive to any sales force.

Words to Sell By

Negative Connotation	*Positive Connotation*
Sell	Own
Buy	Own
Payments	Investment
Sign	Okay/approve
Contract	Agreement
Pay	Invest
Credit app	Customer statement
Give	Pay/buy
Deposit	Partial payment
Demo	Evaluate
Allowance	Pay/buy
Appraisal	Sell
Prove/explain	Share

(continued)

(Continued)

Depreciation	Usage value
Inflation	Improvement cost
Appointment	Get together
Manager	Team leader
Discount	Savings
Asking price	Market value
Deal	Transaction
I'm sorry	Forgive
Why don't we	Let's
Help	Be of service
Plus Tax	And fees
How far apart	How close are we?
Thank you	Congratulations
It's not worth it	Market value
They can't do it	Bypass/why, sure!
Finance man	Biz manager
Finance Company	Lending company
Problem	Challenge
Lady	Name (use Mrs. or Ms.)
Sir	Name (use first name or title)
You're wrong	Truth
Service	No-negative
Today	Now
Lease	Alternative program
Spot delivery	Preferred delivery
Think about this	Evaluate this

You may or may not be one of those lucky few born with a few skills of the communication master. You may have to rededicate yourself daily to fostering these skills into unconscious competencies. Either way, remember one simple rule: forget thyself and know thy client. Ask not what your client can do for you, but what you can do for your client (as long as you are not being codependent!).

When it comes to listening, use the force. And if you're not paying attention, you're not getting paid . . . got it?

Communication Mastery Commission Development Quiz

Anything fewer than 100 percent correct answers requires immediate additional work!

1. _____ out of 10 messages are misunderstood, mistaken, missed, or just plain messed-up in one way or another.

2. In any communication with clients, _____ outsells product knowledge.

3. The facts and claims in your message must always be _____.

4. If you are early, you're a salesperson, if you're on time, you're a genius, and if you're late, you're a _____.

5. Don't be a plastic pink flamingo. Instead, be _____.

6. Don't _____ the value of your product or service.

(*continued*)

(*Continued*)

7. Instead of a _____ _____,
learn to be an *effective* communicator.

8. Make sure your _____ is in agreement
with your words and your tone.

9. When   provoked,   don't   overreact.   Always
_____.

10. The communication skill that outweighs all of the others
is _____.

11. After only _____ words, most salespeople stop listening.

12. Which of the words or phrases listed as ones that shatter
intimacy can you identify that you've recently used and
need to replace?

13. Which intimacy-building words or phrases will you use to
replace the words you identified in #12?

14. Which personality style prefers communication in the version of a novel?

(*continued*)

(*Continued*)

15. Which personality style prefers to be communicated to in bullet points?

16. Which client is best touched with a short story communication style?

17. And which one for laser-focused phrases?

Communication Mastery Quiz Answers

1. Seven

2. Enthusiasm

3. Accurate

4. Bozo

5. Authentic

6. Overinflate

7. Defective elaborator

8. Body language

9. Underrespond

10. Listening

11. Seven

(*continued*)

(Continued)

12. Remember, the truth is good enough

13. Your option

14. Thinkers

15. Directors

16. Socializers

17. Relaters

7

Presentation Mastery

Y ou may be surprised to know it doesn't matter one iota what size or type of audience you have, whether it's someone standing in front of you alone, a small company's board of directors, a large audience, a single person on the phone, or a conference call in front of 50 people—the recipe for a valuable presentation always requires the same ingredients.

In fact, let me share with you an illustration that underscores this universal claim, a very rude awakening that I experienced during my early days of public speaking. I had been lecturing groups for about a year and thought I was really good . . . until one day in Charlotte, North Carolina, when I spoke to a group of about 70 people about personal development skills.

Just three hours before my speech, notable sales industry figure and author of the best-selling book *The Sales Bible* Jeffrey Gitomer called me to say, "Hey Bauer, I know you're speaking tonight. Do you mind if I come in and sit in on it and critique you, give you some constructive criticism?" I said, "No, Jeffrey, that's fine. I'd be more than happy to have you come in and hear what you have to say afterward. Anything you can help me with it would be greatly appreciated." Just one or two minutes before my seven o'clock speech, the great Jeffrey Gitomer walked in carrying a legal pad that was just shy of the size of South Dakota. Without a word, he perched himself in the very back row and pulled out a pen.

After my one-hour power-hour performance, I made several social rounds with the guests, and then I humbly sat down with Jeffrey. I hadn't even really met him yet, and the anticipation of the moment brought on a little sweaty-palm syndrome. Despite the slight nervousness, I became knighted by his observations and feedback; in fact, it made such an impact on my career that it qualifies as a defining moment in my life. The most resounding statement Jeffrey made was "You didn't engage the audience within the first sixty seconds."

"What?" I was surprised. "What do you mean I wasn't engaging the audience? I was telling them everything I know."

"No, no, no," he replied. "You've got to *engage* them by asking them a question, telling them a story, getting them engaged in the story, and [encouraging] them to respond to you—versus you just giving your pitch."

I haven't gotten that "song" out of my head ever since. To this day—because of Jeffrey's statement—I kick off every presentation with the knowledge that I had better engross that audience with a question or discussion within the first 30-to-60 seconds—or I may lose my message in a sea of drifting minds.

Let the advice Jeffrey Gitomer gave me over 15 years ago ring in your head now and help you become aware of a potentially disappointing fact: you're probably not engaging your clients. Engaging does not mean *pitching* them; rather, it requires **getting them *involved*** in a very high level of discussion about your product, offering, or service. You want them to think about what you're saying and respond, not tune you out.

Let me reiterate what a major connection killer failing to listen can be. Trust me—your ears work better when your mouth is closed. The prospect will only have a chance to give you feedback if put your pitch on pause. By listening to your client or prospect, you're more likely to hear what they need, figure out how to meet that need, and close the sale.

Have you ever tried driving alongside another car in the same lane? Someone inevitably ends up driving off the road, right? That's what it's like when two people talk at once, too—and because of that, another major presentation violation is **talking over people** on a frequent basis. It's a nasty habit. Yet since you don't know what you don't know, you probably don't even realize you're doing it. Overall, I think you would be surprised if I came into your office, got hooked up on a headset and shadowed phone calls with you. You'd be amazed to discover how many dinks and scratches are on what you thought was a perfect pearl of a pitch.

The instruction to engage with clients is the perfect segue to introducing the other metered events in a presentation—whether face-to-face or on the phone—as they relate to your audience. Various researchers and speaking organizations have proven over the years that within the first minute of a speech, 30 percent of the audience has decided that they don't like you. It could be the way you speak, the way you dress, the way your hair is parted . . . all sorts of things that seemingly don't make much sense. But logical or not, one-third of the audience has made an unfavorable judgment about you within the first minute of your presentation. And, what's even worse, by the time you reach the first five minutes, *another* 30 percent doesn't like you! So, 6 out of 10 people have decided that—for whatever reason—they don't like you . . . all during the first five minutes.

This theory applies to phone presentations as well; in other words, if you make 10 phone calls, it's likely that 6 out of 10 people won't like you within the first 5 minutes of your phone call. Your mission—whether in person or over the phone—is to bring that 60 percent back into the fold so that by the end of the presentation—whether it was 5 minutes, 20 minutes, or an hour long—everybody likes you enough for you to succeed with a soft but certain close. This notion also connects to your notes from the Communication Mastery chapter about building intimacy with a person or group. (You did take notes, didn't you?)

One way to get people to like you is to connect with them; this will often make the difference between closing a sale and failing to do so. In fact, the number *one* reason you're going to receive "No" as an answer is, quite honestly, that your clients don't like you. And they probably don't like you because you're *not* connecting with them. So how do we make clients like us? How do we create that bond?

Although your presentation content does have some weight here, it's the way in which you deliver that information that tips the scales in your favor. This comes across through body language and voice quality; in fact, 93 percent of all communication is nonverbal. So try using body language, even if you're on the phone. Believe it or not, it will affect your voice quality.

Although a lack of connection is the biggest reason that you hear "No" from them, it's certainly not the only card in the deck. Another reason you might fail to close the deal is the result of an incorrect or incomplete explanation of whatever it is that you're selling. One simple way to avoid making this mistake: keep your audience in mind when you are creating your presentation, and realize that they don't know your offering as well as you do. Tell them—without sounding condescending—exactly what they need to know to prompt them to say "Yes!"

The reason for a negative response may come from some unpleasant nostalgia. This takes place when your presentation triggers the memory of a stressful past sales experience for the client. They may be reminded of a previous business transaction that went sour, which prompts them to view you and your presentation from a somewhat distressed mindset. This can significantly distract them from hearing—and appreciating—you speaking about the benefits of your product, offering, or service.

However, this does not have to happen to you. Learning how to present means discovering how to recognize—and avoid—those three poison darts that deliver a "No": a client's dislike of you, an inadequate explanation of what you're selling, or bad memories of a past sales experience.

Many years ago, I cut my sales teeth in the car business. That experience gave me the opportunity to witness the bad habits of countless salespeople—habits that immediately elicit unpleasant memories for customers. Though every industry has salespeople with poor social habits, the car business is notorious for this trend. You pull up on a car lot and the vultures in white polyester shirts with the sleeves rolled up swoop down on you and puff a cigarette cloud right above your head the moment you get out of your car. Thus begins your dreadful sales experience—one that you remember every time you go car shopping. So we learn from this: don't do the things that people don't like that everyone else is doing. And if you're part of the "everyone else" who's doing them—*stop*.

Another common pitfall is a lack of any visuals in your presentations. Visual presentations help explain and make it less likely that your audience will zone out, begin to wonder what time you'll wrap it up, what to have for supper, errands they have to run, or relatives they need to call back—*anything* but what you are telling them.

Another presentation infraction is a lack of stories or examples. You don't want to miss out on explaining *why* your audience should do business with you or your company. You can easily accomplish this by using an aid for the client to envision herself benefiting from your product, offering, or service. The same as with visuals, stories and examples give your audience something to latch on to and help them understand how it can meet their needs.

Another presentation flaw is a lack of third party evidence. Your audience might be thinking "Why should I take *this* person's word for it? After all, they're selling it; of course they think it's great!" Solid, well-presented, third party evidence—testimonials from previous and current clients, for example—can help you overcome those objections, and convince your client that they can—and indeed, *should*—take your word for it. Although some members of the financial industry will have company compliance departments that prohibit the use of third party evidence, you can speak generally about examples of the benefits. Be sure to keep the examples vague, but supportive of your presentation.

Last but not least, the presentation violation of which so many salespeople are guilty is failing to have copies of "One-Page Sales Sheets" (discussed in detail in Chapter 5: Sales Tools) on hand.

These sheets are another way to present third party evidence and provide other supporting information to help you engage your client and close the sale.

Reasons for Hearing "No"

- Client doesn't like you
- Incomplete or inaccurate presentation
- Unpleasant memories
- Lack of visuals
- Lack of stories or examples
- Lack of third party evidence
- Lack of sales sheets

So while graphs, third party evidence, and stories are important instruments in your presentation, don't forget the help that's offered by your other inherent allies: body language and voice quality. There has been research conducted as far back as the 1930s on the impact of a person's message, and everything points back to this truth: the impact of your message comes from these three sources—your body language, your voice quality, and your words. Body language—which is mostly facial expressions—comprises 55 percent of your message's effectiveness. In second place, with 38 percent impact, is voice quality: the pitch, pace, and ability you use to articulate your message. In last place—with only 7 percent of the impact of a message—are your words. Though it's the area in which people tend to spend the most time, words carry the least authority. I occasionally receive e-mails from salespeople asking me to edit some of their writing, and to make some suggestions on a power word here or there. Despite the fact that I want to help improve their presentations, I have to tell them that altering one or two words won't change a thing.

Yes, words have the least amount of importance. I have a copy of *Words That Sell* sitting on my desk in my office, which I use frequently to strengthen my language. However, it's vital to realize that words are just one of three key communication instruments—and again, the one that matters the least. Remember: 93 percent of the impact of your message has everything to do with nonverbal expressions—body language and voice quality. Despite this fact, most salespeople, sales managers, and business owners invest their time on words.

You can distinguish and help both yourself and your clients and prospects by paying more attention to your body language and voice inflection. Believe it or not, it's not just what you're seeing in body language; it's what you're *not* seeing that makes a difference. For example, when you're having a face-to-face meeting with a client, you might not consciously ask yourself, "Why is the client not smiling?" The client may not realize that they're wondering, "Why is the salesperson slouching?" But despite our failure to deliberately acknowledge things like a missing smile or poor posture, both of us will notice these things, and they *will* influence the course of the presentation. They somehow seep into the subconscious and either pollute or enhance the message.

When you can utilize body language as taught in *Sales Mastery*, every moment you spend with others will become more valuable. And because you're in sales, you can turn that valuable time into tangible profits. Body language is the key; it is the highest level of communication that contributes to your success. And the best part is—it's *easy*! As long as you smile, you can forget everything else, since research has shown us that smiling and facial expressions have the most substantial impact on body language transmission and reception. And always remember: this applies to both face-to-face communication *and* phone sales.

Let me give you an example of how body language, voice inflection, and words work together. Many years ago, I consulted for an energy company in Dallas, Texas, that relied heavily on phone sales—50 to 75 to 100 dials each day. During my consultation, a Korean man named Young Kim applied for a position at the company. Since I was in charge of their recruiting efforts, I called the CEO and told him, "I interviewed this guy for you. His sales assessment looks good, he dresses well, he's a man of integrity and a hard worker, but the challenge is that he can't speak English."

The CEO replied, "No way! We're not going to do anything with him." Thirty days later, Young Kim called me up and said "Mr. Bauer, please give me one more chance." We brought him in for a second interview during which the CEO essentially told him the following: "Mr. Kim, we're going to give you thirty days to make a sale. If you don't make it in thirty days, then that's it." In short, he had a month to prove himself.

So they got Mr. Kim started in the training program, and I didn't really hear anything else until about his 21st day with the company. That was when the CEO called me and said, "Chuck, you gotta come in here and take care of this guy from Korea. He's made absolutely no sales." I told the CEO, "I'll come in and see what I can do." Before my coaching session with Young, I reflected on my knowledge of body language, voice quality, and words and thought "Well, I can change two of those things; one of them, I can't. I can change his voice quality and his body language, even if I am unable to help or change his words."

So I went to Young Kim's office, took him into a conference room, and told him, "Young, you've got five days to make a sale or you're out of here—so here's what we can do. We can work on your body language, and we can work on your voice quality. However, there's really nothing I can do about your inability with the English language. But I can see that you're trying—so we can change up a couple of things."

We got settled in the conference room, where I fired up YouTube and showed Young Kim a Nido Qubein video. For the seven minutes of the video, Young watched the video *without* the audio on, watching only Nido's body language intently. I felt confident that Young would benefit from this, because there's nobody better in the world at demonstrating body language than Nido. Even though Young was only making phone calls and not conducting any face-to-face sales, he still concentrated on what he saw. As the video continued, he began to realize that he needed to alter his body language.

When the video ended, I proceeded to coach Young with the following advice: "Your voice has to be powerful. Throttle it with command, and stand up. Standing releases the diaphragm, adding much-needed oxygen and thus providing more horsepower for vocal control. Be sure to add gestures to emphasize your words, which will make your tone more dynamic and expressive."

Young started to take notes, and I could see that he was really intent on studying and making himself coachable. I then ran the same video again, with the audio on this time. Not only did he get to see Nido's body movements the second time around; he also got to hear the words, pitch, pace, and articulation. At the end of our session, I turned to Young and said, "If you can do what Nido does, you'll overcome the fact that your English is broken and not very understandable." Young said "Okay, Mr. Bauer, I'm going to go home and practice, drill, and rehearse."

That night, Young went home and practiced in front of his wife, Sung, then in front of the mirror, then in front of his wife again. The next day, one of the managers called me and said, "Come by here if you've got a second. You've got to see Young Kim." So I went to the office, walked down the hallway, looked around the corner, and, sure enough, there was Young standing up, looking and sounding like a nearly identical model of Nido Qubein—right down to his facial expressions!

The point here is this: Young was coachable, took copious notes, was really intent on changing his pitch, and watched videos at home. While watching, he isolated the video and audio portions in order to get each part right. If you take these actions right now, you too will learn what Young learned from Nido Qubein, and you'll be able to incorporate these lessons into your presentations immediately.

I'm sure you want to know the end of the story for Young. That experience changed both his sales career and his life. He went from making no sales to making his first that very week. He went on to break sales records, contribute a significant portion of his salary from sales to his church, and received a promotion to manager. I still bring him in front of audiences around Dallas to prove a very important point: when you have people who can speak English as perfectly as you and I can, you can certainly make sales like a guy who speaks broken English.

Though power is found in pitch, pace, and articulation, the most useful advice for presenting—which I also learned from Qubein—is this: you want to speak as if you're reading aloud from a Dr. Seuss book. "Dr. Seuss?" you're probably wondering with surprise, thinking of books like *How the Grinch Stole Christmas*, *The Cat in the Hat*, and *One Fish, Two Fish*. But imagine if for a moment you had a group of children sitting on the floor in front of you. It's your job to read the Dr. Seuss book, gain their attention, and keep them tuned in. So what do you do? Well, if you're like most people, you put the book in one hand and open it up so that the kids can see both pages. Then in order to hold the children's attention, we slow our speech down. Most people naturally speak too quickly. So start by pointing at the words and reducing the speed at which you speak. Articulate your words carefully to get your point across. You will want to use the same approach with slides and visual expressions in face-to-face presentations, audience presentations, and phone presentations. The same dynamic works equally well in all situations.

A great way to emphasize a particular word or phrase is to go silent right before you say it. You've heard of the pregnant pause; this is a very effective tactic to use when you're in front of a prospect, while on a phone, or during a webinar presentation. You may see many members of a large audience lean in toward you if you go silent for a moment. It's a very effective method to use to become a better salesperson and presenter.

A lot of presenters fail to acknowledge the fact that there is a period at the end of every sentence. (See it there?) Many blow right by this vital component of a structured sentence. The period means one thing: S-T-O-P. Use my P.S.P. strategy, which stands for Pause, Silence, and Patience. Pause. Take a breath. Be patient for a moment. Watch how the audience listens to the silence, then observe how they wait for your next word. Creating these gaps and using proper pitch, pace, and articulation is a technique that we in Chuck Bauer Sales Training call "Seussing." I will give you some speed requirements and tell you how to put this all together at the end of this chapter.

As you're learning these skill components, you'll realize we can all learn from the other speakers we've heard over the years. The following is a list of people I consider to be top speakers, in no particular order: Nido Qubein, Jim Rohn, President Ronald Reagan, President John F. Kennedy, Martin Luther King Jr., James Spader, and Jack LaLanne. While James Spader might not make a lot of other people's "best speakers" list, it's compelling to watch a recording of television show *Boston Legal*—particularly without audio—to witness his body language brilliance. Then add audio and review it. When Spader is acting in a courtroom scene, his pitch, pace, articulation, and body language are at the highest levels of effectiveness. Who are your favorite speakers? If you can't think of any, try to come up with a list and watch them on YouTube. It will not cost you anything but your time, and what you learn about presentations, pitch, pace, articulation, and body language will prove more than valuable.

Client's Believability Scale

Everything in this chapter up to this point affects the Client's Believability Scale, or C.B.S. As you can see in Figure 7.1, the C.B.S. is displayed as a stoplight. This commonplace object represents the tactics you are using and lets you quickly identify progress and professionalism—or the lack thereof. As in stoplights, the red means *stop*—cease any behavior that keeps clients from believing in you. The yellow zone indicates that while some level of truth is present, there is also room for improvement. Green means that you have achieved the highest level of credibility from your client's perspective.

Let's start at the bottom and work our way up. If you are a salesperson, sales manager, or business owner, and you are *only* speaking and talking to your clients and prospects, you are in the red zone—which means that you need to simply stop talking and pitching. The red zone is where you have the least credibility for

C.B.S. Clients' Believability Scale

HIGHEST	· Talk · Visual · Story	· Personality Style · 3rd Party · Client Engagement
MEDIUM	· Talk · Visual · Story	
LOWEST	· Talk	

www.chuckbauer.com • www.cbsalestools.com

FIGURE 7.1

your clients, where the voice inside their head is likely to be saying, "I wonder what time it is in Hong Kong." The voice may also be saying "I have fear, uncertainty, and doubt!" To get to the yellow zone of believability, support your claims about the product or service that you're offering with a visual aid *and* a story or example. At this point, the voice inside the client's head has changed to saying, "Now, what to have for dinner . . . Oh! Wait! What was it that he just said?" To move on to green—the most effective and professional level—you need to include the preceding pitch, visual, and story, as well as some third party visual evidence to get the client fully engaged. Remember the fishing story from a previous chapter? That really exemplifies how the Client's Believability Scale works. You can go to www.chuckbauer.com/cbs and print the graphic out so you can use it as a memory tool in your office, cubicle, or during training sessions.

Let's take it one step further. One of the most powerful statements that the Chinese philosopher Confucius ever made as it relates to *your* presentations was the following: "I hear, and I forget; I see, and I remember; *I do, and I understand*." If you merely speak to your audience, they'll remember you for about five minutes. If you speak and offer them a visual illustration, they'll remember you for an hour. And if you *engage* them—as Jeffrey Gitomer instructed me to do back in 1995—then they'll understand, and they'll remember you even tomorrow. And if you didn't manage to close the deal today, you had better have impressed them enough so that they think about you tomorrow. Otherwise, your competitor may be the next "expert" they listen to. However, there will be times when you *are* simply talking to your clients; there's no way around this. In these situations, you can easily structure your pitch into what I call an S.S.P.—a Standard Sales Pitch, as mentioned in the Sales Tools chapter. This script has three elements, and it doesn't matter if your pitch is 5 minutes, 30 minutes, or 60 minutes long: all of the components will apply.

Begin typing your brainstorm: open by using logic and paint the "big picture" of what's in it for your clients. With big broad strokes, fill the middle portion of your speech with emotion. Then, last but not least, close with logic again. Use a six-foot push-broom brush to paint these stories and structure your pitch. It is fairly easy; you can have three main points with three bullet points each, so that all you really need to do is remember nine significant things. Remember the path from logic, emotion, and back to logic to finally close it.

The next thing you need to do is to put the information in either a script form or a series of bullets, or both. You'll have three main points (logic–emotion–logic) for a bulleted script, each with three subpoints. Then you close and ask for the order. This simple structure is easy to remember. If you try to include more categories, you'll risk overloading your client with too much information—which I can guarantee you they won't remember. As long as you pitch with the sequence of logic–emotion–logic, this strategy will appeal to all personality styles. Though you will want to determine which structure—a script, bullet points, or a combination of both—works best for you, most companies have a policy or procedure in place for scripting—so stick to it. The script will also help members of the financial industry remain in compliance; in any other industry, it helps maintain consistency in portraying high levels of professionalism to your clients. Regardless of what method you use, remember that brevity works best. (See Figure 7.2.)

Standard Sales Pitch

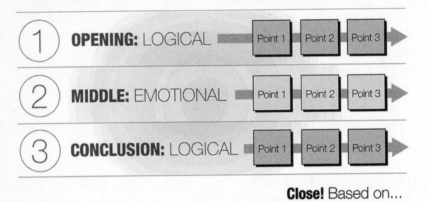

www.chuckbauer.com • www.cbsalestools.com

FIGURE 7.2

Since I happen to also be an instrument-rated private pilot, I have included a diagram of something that's known as an "instrument approach plate" at my home airport here in Dallas, Texas, to strengthen my argument about the necessity of having an S.S.P. (see Figure 7.3). Notice the black marks on the graphic, every one of which has a significant meaning. Typically, each mark indicates a spot where an accident has occurred in the past. By sticking to a script, pilots diminish the risk of hurting themselves. But any time they drift off, it's usually an issue.

The same holds true in sales. If you deviate too far from the script, you risk plummeting to certain sales death. So find that script and become it and own it. You might discover that while you can veer off slightly, safety remains in sticking to the script.

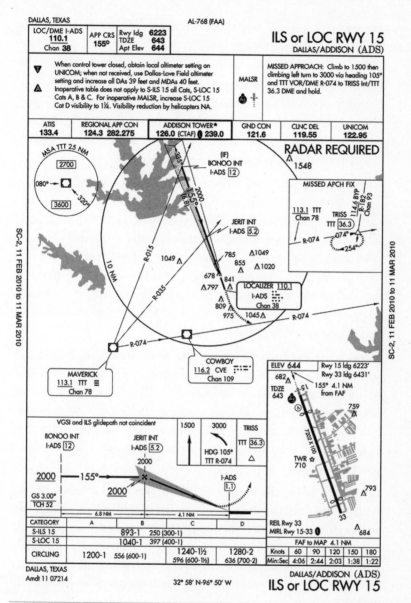

FIGURE 7.3

Here are 10 step-by-step tips to giving an effective presentation that audiences will remember:

1. **Create a memorable brand**. For example, my website layout, colors, icons, and data layout are all congruent with my presentation material. You need to blend your brand ID throughout to be at the peak of professionalism. Be professionally consistent with your messages and presentations.

2. **Command attention**. When I'm meeting with clients face-to-face, it's easy for me to command attention; I'm always in a suit and tie, my nails are manicured, my shoes are shined, and I have presence. I command attention when I walk into a room. I am standing up straight, shoulders back. However, even if I'm on a phone call, I manage to keep this up—based on how I'm dressed, the body language I use, the projection of command in my voice, and using that boost of self-esteem that dressing professionally affords me.

3. **Show interest in your prospects and clients**. Regardless of whether I'm presenting to an audience or a single person, one of my opening questions is always, "Tell me about your specific needs and challenges as they relate to your sales." Adapt that question to your industry to let clients or prospects know that you're concerned about their needs. Then the discussion you want will begin.

4. **Organize yourself**. Have everything prepared in advance and ready to go. Try to predict any possible pushback or objections, and organize yourself to be ready at a second's notice to handle whatever comes up. In addition to this, of course, as you already know, I'm a big advocate for everybody using iPads in their sales processes. So make sure to get organized, electronically and otherwise.

5. **Translate everything you do into a benefit**. Word your presentation in a way that makes it easy for clients and prospects to see what they will gain. Explain every step in your sales

process as "This is your benefit; this is your solution." Clients and prospects will pay attention to this. Your audience isn't buying that particular product or service; they're buying a way to make their lives easier/better/more enjoyable.

6. **Ask questions that elicit discussion.** While on a particular coaching call, a client of mine made a big to-do about open-ended questions and closed-ended questions, a comparison that's discussed in most run-of-the-mill sales books. An open-ended question, of course, requires discussion, while closed-ended questions usually elicit a yes or no answer. However, you should know this: the salespeople who are getting up in those intimate zones don't worry about an open-ended question or a closed-ended question. Regardless of the kinds of queries they use, they're habitually having good discussions with their clients—which is what *you* need to do. Have the kind of dialogue that enhances your connection and eliminates F.U.D.

7. **Get to the point.** First, make sure that you *have* a point. (Some salespeople are ramblers, and don't have a point. Or, worse, their sales discussions remind me of a tennis match.) Whatever it is, get to the point—and keep it short. Your clients will appreciate your succinctness.

8. **Engage the client.** Encourage them to write things out. Make your way through the questions and have a quality conversation. Ask them to repeat their most important concerns and issues back to you, so that you're sure that you're covering what matters most to them.

9. **Be real.** Be real. Be real.

10. **Show enthusiasm.** I have said it before, and I'll say it again here: enthusiasm will *always* beat out product knowledge. You can always get the details about anything you might not know later on, but your clients won't even have these additional questions if you don't show excitement for your product or service in the first place.

Avoid Speeding

As promised earlier, let's now discuss presentation speed as it relates to pitch, pace, and articulation. This is called a "listenable rate" of speech. There is a preferred speed of communication that allows the listener to more fully receive the information we're sending. The ideal speed is 140 to 160 words per minute, and if we practice speaking at that pace, we develop the ability to connect with our clients, gain intimacy, and enhance our ability to close sales.

Most people don't realize how fast they speak if they don't have a gauge that lets them know. A lot of salespeople with whom I work on speech improvement typically speak at a pace of over 200 words per minute. That's like going 80 mph in a 20 mph school zone—*danger*! A client will have a lot of trouble understanding you at this pace and will almost certainly miss major portions of your presentation. Though it may be difficult to slow down on your first attempt, you need to make a concentrated effort to do so—because your sales success depends on it. There's one particular tactic I've used with salespeople who struggle to speak at a less-hurried pace: I've actually mounted a graphic on the wall in their office that displays a police officer with a radar gun to remind them to slow down (see Figure 7.4).

www.chuckbauer.com • www.cbsalestools.com

FIGURE 7.4

I've included two paragraphs at the end of this section that are used to practice the "listenable rate of speech." Read the paragraphs aloud to recognize where and how to vary your pitch, pace, and articulation. You should articulate the words in italics and bold font, and find key words in the material you're speaking or reading. Some of the words might unconsciously prompt you to do certain things; for example, seeing the word *fast* in front of another word might cause you to speak quickly, whereas the word *slow* can serve as a reminder to slow down. And remember: a period means *stop*; it doesn't mean continue speaking until you asphyxiate and turn blue.

Read these paragraphs a few times, and then recite out loud—preferably in front of someone, such as a sales buddy—which will help by putting pressure on you. You'll likely go much too fast the first time you recite, so focus on articulating the words. Once you feel that you're becoming a master at it, record and time yourself. Since the paragraphs combined are exactly 160 words long, it will be easy for you to score yourself. Play it back to review your use of pitch, pace, and articulation; remember, practice makes perfect.

I want you to perfect the rate at which you speak, and become as proficient as Nido Qubein. Becoming a better communicator will help you gain intimacy with clients and allow you to Seuss every person with whom you come in contact. Instead of just being a presenter, you will transform yourself into a professional persuader. And you will earn a well-deserved raise. So grab a stopwatch and let's get started. Here are your two practice paragraphs.

As a representative of <your company name>, it is important that you speak *clearly*. That means that you must *articulate*. It also means that you *must* speak so that you can be *understood*. Although there is no set rate of speech, most expert speakers talk at between one-hundred-and-forty and one-hundred-and-sixty words per minute. That is a good speed for verbal communication. It is not *too fast* to be understood. It does not give the listener the impression that you are under pressure *nor is it too sloooooooow*.

The one-hundred-sixty word rate adds *an element of dignity* to your voice. The one-hundred-sixty word rate also gives a *sound image* to your audience that *establishes* both you and <your company name> as *efficient and well-organized.* To give the audience the kind of impression of yourself and <your company name> *that you wish*, speak correctly, and speak at one-hundred-and-sixty—that's one-hundred-and-sixty words per minute.

So how did you do?

Memorize Your Chorus Line

Another vital component of every presentation is using a closing "chorus line"—a phrase or question that you remember when you get flustered, even lose your head completely, and can't recall anything else. This reflexive statement will also help you to overcome objections and deal with conflict. You will be able to remember the closing chorus line because it's very simple. It's a basic statement or question that asks for the order: "Based on what I've shared with you, are you ready to proceed?" I work with sales managers across the country who tell me that their chief complaint with salespeople is that *they do not ask for the order*. I have observed myself while listening to live sales calls or attending face-to-face presentations wherein the salesperson conducts a great 15-minute presentation on their product, offering, or service—and they don't even ask for an order at the end. What was the point of all that presenting? Just to take up space and hang out? Of course not! We're selling! We have to ask for the order! State your closing chorus line!

You need to do a few things to make sure your chorus line is effective. First, memorize it. Then practice, drill, and rehearse. Make it a reflex, as though it comes out of your mouth on its own. Second, develop two chorus lines based on the original—one for feelings-based people, and the other for logic-or-ego-based people. To simplify: every one of your chorus lines should start out with the words "Based on" and then continue with one of the following variations: "Based on what I've just shared with you, are you ready to proceed?," "Based on what I've just shown you, are you ready to purchase this product?," "Based on your positive responses in the last thirty minutes of our conversation, are you ready to sign the contract?" That's all there is to it. So even when you can't remember anything else, remember your chorus line.

Face-to-Face Presentations

The last thing we're going to discuss in this chapter is face-to-face presentations, which are pretty simple as long as you make sure that you're organized ahead of time. You've got to be prepared and have some preexisting knowledge of the prospect or client with whom you will be meeting. You must develop a very clear understanding of their specific needs and challenges in advance of the meeting. While this doesn't give you the green light to spend countless hours doing a bunch of over-the-top, crazy research—a tactic that I call revenue aversion—you should know a little bit about what you're going into so that you can meet their needs, solve their challenges, overcome their objections, and close the sale. Be sure to check even obvious items, such as making sure you have GPS directions to the office building, and using and maximizing Outlook by checking that all appointments are automatically confirmed.

Next, what about your arrival time? Do you arrive early? On time? You arrive *on time*. When walking into the office, use your unique approach and out-of-the-box tactics to distinguish yourself. Don't be like all the other salespeople in the world. Dress as nicely as possible and don't use the excuse, "They dress down in their office, so I can, too." No. Go one level above this. Make sure your shoes are polished, your clothes are pressed, your hair is clean and neat, and that everything about you looks right (even the manicured nails that I discussed in the first chapter—for both men *and* women.) When you come up to the gatekeeper, smile, introduce yourself, and always have three secret weapons with you: two copies of your Main Point Cards, and chocolate. Hand the gatekeeper both cards: one for him or her, and one for them to take back to the person with whom you are meeting. The chocolate is comfort food, your secret weapon for the gatekeeper.

Once you've been greeted, you will be offered a seat. *Don't ever sit down*. Always remain standing and in close proximity to the gatekeeper. The fact that this person sees you still standing will put a little bit of positive pressure on them to make sure the appointment is kept for the proper time. Stand with your hands behind your back or at your sides; one hand in your pocket is appropriate, but not both. Your presence and body language will say a lot by answering these subliminal questions that the gatekeeper and person with whom you're meeting might have: "Is this person confident? Does he or she come from a company with whom we want to work? Is this salesperson different from all the rest?" They will begin judging you the moment you first step through the door, so you need to be confident when you walk in and have all your sales tools and techniques working for you. Don't forget: the gatekeeper and the person you met *will* without a doubt talk about you after you leave.

You also need to be making some quick judgments of your own. Let's say that your client or prospect walks out to meet you. You need to smile as the person approaches you. If the client or prospect is an ego-based person, then it's going to be a handshake situation; however, if they approach you with more open body language, then that person is probably a hugger. Don't sit there and let your ego give the message "Oh, I would never hug anybody." Remember—you're catering to their personality and preferences, not your own. Get beyond your own unease, and give a feelings-focused person a little side hug or a pat on the arm. It's not a big deal; in fact, it's a sign of sales maturity that will benefit *both* of you. However, when in doubt, just shake hands.

When you go into the conference room or office or wherever you're going to meet, do not ever, ever, *ever* sit at the head of the table. Sit in the middle where you can speak, see, and show things to everyone present easily. Don't ask where to sit; just go to the other side of the conference table and sit down. When a woman enters the room, always stand up as a matter of courtesy and politeness, regardless of the era in which you were raised. Do the same when a woman leaves the room, and always watch your manners.

There is also the challenge of technology to manage. When I walk into a conference room, I always have my laptop with me. Don't worry that you're taking up time if you need an extra minute to boot up your equipment; everybody is accustomed to that.

When your technological tools are ready, break the ice, start the discussion, and begin to entertain great questions with these people. My standard opening line is "Now that we're all here together, would you do me a favor and share with me your specific needs and challenges?" And that's it; I then let each person simply answer the question I've asked. While I'm listening intently to their responses, I'm also taking notes and classifying their personality style. Why? Well, we've already discussed it in the Personality Selling chapter. But even more specifically, I need to make sure that I know what their personality style is to determine how *to close them*. I'm listening, rather than pitching. I'm seeing how much F.U.D. is present in the room. Where do their fears, uncertainty, and doubt reside? I'm compiling all this information both in my laptop and my brain, so that I can quickly retrieve it and use it to solve their issues and close the deal.

Once you've broken the ice and led a constructive discussion, it is the appropriate time to whip out that always-beneficial phrase, "Tell me about you." And when they've finished responding, you've got to determine if they've really shared everything that they're going to share. You don't want to cut them off or stop them if you think they have more to tell you. Once you truly believe that they've told you everything they have to say, you then provide a solution that matches your product, offering, or service to their needs or wants according to their personality style.

Let's now discuss what happens when you're in the midst of your pitch. You want to create the solution for your client. You should have four rounds of ammo ready: your Fast Facts Profile sheet (the one-page sheet that talks about you, the company, and the product), your testimonial sheet of third party evidence backing up your company (unless you have a compliance department that forbids it), an overcoming objections sheet of third party information that kills any potential protests, and a legal pad for your prospects to write down questions. Don't forget what Confucius said: "I hear and I forget; I see and I remember; I do and I understand." So *get them engaged*. When you start talking about the company or the product, turn that Fast Facts Profile sheet around to walk them through the main points. If you have to go to the overcoming objections sheet, turn that sheet around and display the information, Vanna White style. Always try to speak and show at the same time. If your lips are moving, you had better be pointing!

My sales model requires that I always conduct two meetings to conclude a sale, whereas your model might require a one-call close. I initially engage clients in face-to-face interaction to build their confidence. Then I create a formal proposal—which I always call a *solution*—in a portfolio, and bring it back to the clients at a scheduled time. This is the point at which you might need to ask for a straightforward close.

Always assume the close when you reach the conclusion. I take it for granted that I'm going to get the business for every presentation that I do and every phone call that I make. That's just how it is with me, and that's how it needs to be with you. Do I get every deal? No, of course not. I use the opportunities where I do not close, though, to learn, tweak, and adjust—as you should be doing. But the fact of the matter is that I go in with guns blazing and know ahead of time that I'm going to get that deal.

Remember to "sing" your chorus line during your close. If you lose your head and don't know what to do or where to go, make use of that saying: "Based on what I've just shared with you. . . ." Then finish rolling into the close and be quiet. If the answer is an affirmative, great; make sure any paperwork your client has to fill out is easy. Use a highlighter to indicate important sections, and don't make an "x" where they should sign, since it has somewhat of a negative connotation. Instead, use a check mark—a subliminal mark of approval—near the areas they need to sign. Use those Post-it notes as well to indicate signature areas or other critical information.

However, it's become a high-tech world, as we all know: if you have an iPad that has DocuSign features, you can have them sign electronically and take care of the paperwork right then and there.

Here is another sales surprise: thanking your new clients for their business actually makes it sound like your thank you is self-serving—so don't ever say "Thank you." Replace it with "Congratulations." They've just confirmed that they're going to improve their business and/or lives in a significant way by purchasing from you, so reaffirm that they've made a decision worth acknowledging! As you're getting ready to conclude and leave, remind them of why they chose your product, offering, or service. I always like to tell people, "You will wake up tomorrow glad that you chose me to be your sales coach," "... glad that I'm going to do that seminar for you," "... glad that I'm going to do that consulting project for you." I express the way I want people to feel after my presentations—to have their inner voice saying, "Tomorrow all of my sales needs and challenges are going to be solved by Sales Coach Chuck." Finally, end with a B.R.P.P.—Buyers' Remorse Prevention Package—to ward off any lingering negativity they may have after they've made their decision.

Keep in mind, however, that your presentation doesn't end the day that you close the sale. The aftercare continues through the active T.O.M.A. campaign that you will use to continue to take care of the client and validate your original presentation. Have you built an impenetrable wall around that client to prevent them from taking their future business anywhere else? Are you the victim of an urban advisory board—family, friends, and coworkers who might convince the prospect to change his mind? Are you earning the right to ask for a referral? Are you even aware that doing so reminds the client of the great product or service they now enjoy—which they were convinced to purchase due to your great presentation? Think about these questions. Whether you're face-to-face or on the phone, answer these questions for yourself and use your responses to fan the flames of action—and your presentation will lay the foundation for your future. (See Figure 7.5.)

www.chuckbauer.com • www.cbsalestools.com

FIGURE 7.5

Presentation Mastery Commission Development Quiz

Anything fewer than 100 percent correct answers requires immediate additional work!

1. What are the two different minute markers for a 30 percent to 60 percent drop-off in attention on the part of those who decide they don't like you?

2. There are three reasons your client would give you a "No." What are those reasons?

    A. _____

    B. _____

    C. _____

3. What's missing from this list of presentation mastery disasters?

    A. No client engagement

    B. Doesn't listen

    (continued)

(*Continued*)

   C. Talks over

   D. _____

   E. No visuals

   F. _____

   G. No third party evidence

   H. _____

4. Fill in the missing word in this quote from Confucius: "I hear and I forget; I see and I remember; I ___ and I understand."

5. 93 percent of our message comes from?

6. What are the four key items to include in the highest level of effective presenting?

7. What are the missing characteristics of including a sales story effectively?

   A. Must have a distinctive message

   B. Climax leading to a resolution

   C. _____

   D. Emotional

   E. _____

   F. Unique

   G. Repeat necessary points

   H. _____

(*continued*)

(Continued)

8. In the structure of a pitch, you want to open with
_____, fill the middle with _____,
and close with _____.

9. The majority of a message is delivered through which of these:
A. Words
B. Tone
C. Body language

10. Out of the 10 key presentation tips, which ones have you identified that you can improve on?

11. How many words per minute is the listenable rate of speech?

12. What is a chorus line?

13. What is *your* chorus line?

Presentation Mastery Quiz Answers

1. After 1 minute, and after 5 minutes
2. A. The client doesn't like you.
   B. You didn't explain it correctly.

(continued)

(*Continued*)

    C. Your presentation triggered a negative past sales experience.

3. D. Pitch instead of discussion

    F. No stories

    H. No use of sales sheets

4. Do

5. Nonverbal communication

6. Talk, visual, story, third-party testimonial

7. C. Be *brief*

    E. Relevant

    H. It's what they remember that counts.

8. Logic, emotion, logic

9. C. Body language

10. Your answer

11. 140 to 160

12. A close that is memorized

13. Your answer

CHAPTER

8

Phone Mastery

Can you imagine living a day in your life without using a phone? Probably not—especially during a time when some people have practically had their phones grafted into their arms as another body part. When are you not on your phone? Our phones aren't just personal instruments anymore; they're the main source of business communication between us and our clients and prospects. If wielded properly, it can be the Excalibur for all salespeople.

However, I've found from my practical experience in the field on a daily basis that most salespeople tend to take this tool for granted and unknowingly misunderstand its importance. After observing thousands of live sales phone calls and face-to-face presentations, I've found that the majority of salespeople just don't get how mighty the phone really is. (See Figure 8.1.)

To that end, this chapter covers the expanse of phone usage as a sales tool—from pre-calling-to-post-calling responsibilities, to speaking with prospects, to particular ways to deal with clients on the phone, to dialing the phone, to not getting through, whether to leave a message. You'll also want to know what steps to take

FIGURE 8.1

with gatekeepers, and why cold calling can become one of your best selling strategies (if you'll make it that way). I'll offer tips to sales managers on how they can be more effective with their sales teams. I meet many sales managers who really don't know how to coach their people on phone calls. One of my top client companies here in Dallas averages well over 8,000 calls *a day* for both outbound and inbound phone calls, whereas another company right down the street might average around 200. However, whatever the number of calls may be, all of the rules of engagement still apply. It's time for a journey into the "phone zone."

So let's start at the very beginning: preparing for effective and purpose-driven phone work. The first thing you'll want to do is to create your script as discussed in the Presentation Mastery chapter. Remember, just like a pilot's written flight plan, this script is your guide for safety and results. The second thing to do is to place a mirror by the phone you'll be using, to make sure you're smiling when you're dialing. As we've already established, facial expressions are the primary way in which body language enhances your tone and your presentation. Remember that 93 percent of the impact of a message comes from nonverbal communication, even when the client is not in front of you. The last thing to remember—though it may sound odd—is to hydrate. Not with caffeine, but with the *right* stuff: water. Good filtered water will hydrate your throat, giving you more horsepower in your voice, not to mention that if you do high-call time each day it helps keep your voice in the mood to perform the proper pitch, pace, and articulation (tips I shared with you in the Presentation Mastery chapter). On my heavier coaching days, I typically drain three or four quarts of filtered water right here in my office while on calls with my students. You can and should do the same thing if you're going to do a lot of phone work. Know this—acid-and-sugar-laced soft drinks take away from your speaking ability.

The next step is to make some mental preparations. What are the three greatest fears that your clients have every time the phone rings? *The first one* is that whoever's on the other end of the line is selling something. *The second* is that the person calling them is going to waste their time. Most people are extremely busy nowadays; they're working at the highest levels possible in order to maximize their time, and they just don't want to talk to salespeople on the phone. The client's *third biggest fear* is that whoever's on that phone is just like the rest of the people who call them—disrespectful, a poor communicator, or calling from a list. These three fears create the "perfect storm" of anxiety in the client or prospect's mind. Remember that you *must* quell those fears immediately upon the point of first contact—whether it is a phone conversation or a voicemail message—in order to get through to that client. It's going to take some work on your part, but you can do it.

How do I eliminate the client's sense of fear during a phone call? I make sure that I have command in my voice. I create an urgent vibe by increasing my verbal speed to about 200 words per minute at the beginning of a call, because I have only seconds to get their attention to let them know that I am *also* extremely busy.

I'll repeat the other person's first name back to them to start the call—something called a "voice up." They'll usually respond by saying, "Yes," and I'll say "Sales Coach Chuck Bauer here. Listen, I'm really busy right now, and I know you are too. Do you have just a quick second?" If you can manage to get that phrase in, it will kill the three aforementioned client fears immediately. To drive this very significant point home in front of an audience, I express it in the following way: "I've only got a few seconds. I've got fifteen people walking through my door today, I have ten other phone calls coming in right now, I'm late for my appointment at the gym, and I have to go get a manicure and a pedicure." Though my audience tends to laugh when I'm speaking to a live group, they also get the point: that is how I make it clear to people that I'm busy. I let them know, through the speed and command in my voice, that I'm not going to be like other people who call them and waste their time. And I simultaneously let them know I'm selling something by introducing myself as "*Sales* Coach Chuck Bauer."

Remember the law of reciprocity and the story of Mac, the owner of the big furniture store in Houston? I had about 10 phone calls with Mac prior to my first point of contact with him—none of which was longer than 45 seconds. In fact, when I took him to lunch the day I met with him in Houston, he kind of laughed about it and said, "Most people just lollygag on the phone with me. But I knew that you and I weren't going to spend much time on the phone, and that's why I took your calls—because I sensed that you were busy, too, and wouldn't waste my time." Now, if your prospects and clients aren't busy, then you don't have to go to that extreme. But you immediately have to kill that fear that you are just like all the other salespeople in the world. You do this by conveying command in your voice and ramping up the urgency to get people's attention. Then quickly let them know you're not going to waste their time and that you're a person on a mission—because you *are*. You are a professional closer, right? You are not calling to visit and waste time, right? Beginning your calls by inquiring about their weekend automatically sets you up as a professional visitor instead of a professional closer—and it triggers clients' memories of all those time-wasting calls they've been on. Immediately get to business and, when complete, *then* do your visiting stuff if you must, if required by *your prospect*.

The greatest Phone Mastery tool that you have is your voice, something that most salespeople don't understand. You can take control of your calls within the first three seconds of the call. So how do you do this? It's simple: stand up! Sitting down in a chair compresses your diaphragm by collapsing your posture, whereas standing up and releasing the diaphragm gives your voice horse-power. Words in and of themselves are of little value; rather, it is your voice quality that the listener first detects. To that end, it's very important that you manipulate your body language for this you-can-trust-me-to-lead-you effect.

The next way to engage your client is to *tell* instead of *ask*. This means that you as the salesperson showcase your expertise in a way that makes it okay to tell people what to do. I frequently encounter salespeople who are too meek and mild with their sales skills; instead of telling people what they need to know, they rely on pleasantries such as "please" and "thank you" and "if you don't mind" and "okay," which all give the impression that the salesperson thinks they're bothering the client. Guess what the main reason is for using this overabundance of pleasantries? Your follow-up skills suffer. If you add this to a lack of advanced sales ability you end up trying to overcompensate for your failure to use a precision-based follow up approach. It is imperative that you let the prospect or client know that you are confident that your product, offering, or service will be a huge benefit to them. If we asked your prospects and clients to rank the top ten characteristics and qualities of the salesperson they'd prefer to deal with, do you really think that "nice" is going to be in that list? Most likely not. I'm not saying this to be mean; I am saying it because awareness of this fact will help you to become a consummate sales professional.

You *must* have an authoritative tone in your voice. One of my sales students, Brian, can really navigate people in a conversation. At the very beginning of each call, he has this distinctive little tinge in his voice that sometimes causes the prospect or client to think they're in trouble when they're not. He eliminates small-talk statements such as "How was your weekend?," "If you don't mind . . . ," "If it's not too much of a bother . . . ," and the nauseating excess of "pleases" and "thank yous." This immediately captivates the client's attention, something that makes Brian one of the masters of the authoritative vocal tone.

How to Address Clients' Fears

- Stand up
- Tell, instead of ask
- Have an authoritative tone
- Establish urgency
- Eliminate lollygagging

Now at this point, you may have addressed the listener's fears, but have you addressed your own? Lack of confidence on your part will always nullify anything you tell a prospect or client, no matter the quality of your information or your product. If they detect fear or tentativeness in your voice, that's *all* they will hear, and then you're toast! So how do you keep anxiety at bay? Practice. Drill. Rehearse. Attain confidence, and lose your fear. It begins with feeling comfortable with your discussions, your pitch, your voice messages, your follow-up—every part of your calling process. And from that comfort level, your confidence multiplies.

How can you be certain that you are creating the quality of sales professionalism over the phone? Make a recording of yourself. Play it back and make detailed notes on what you observe. Do you sound like a sales wimp or sales warrior? Are you confident in your information and answers, or does your voice sound vague and debatable? Do you pause before significant words? Do you present irrefutable evidence and use the Client's Believability Scale to your advantage? Do you hesitate before answering a client's question, thereby spoiling the impression of confidence? Even if you're leaving voicemail messages, record those calls and give your managers access to them so they can offer you feedback. Sales managers at companies that do a lot of phone work should record their salespeople's calls—because those calls directly affect the sales foundation. Call reviews are the diagnostic panel by which management is able to determine the type of coaching that's needed to produce a better revenue-generating workforce.

The goal of phone messages is, of course, to get a call back at some point. You need to remember the game of sales, so guess what—leaving a trail of sequential voicemail messages is not going to work. In today's sales world, clients are much more mature than 10 or 20 years ago. The students I coach one-on-one know that if they still haven't received a response after leaving a second message, then they are to choose a different method of communication. If you simply continue to leave multiple messages, your prospects and clients are not going to call you back; you now seem like all the others who are doing that already. You have very little chance of getting a client callback after a time-wasting message stream.

When you *do* leave a voicemail, do not leave any information that might prompt a client or propose to make any decisions. Oh, the woe I feel when I witness a sales call in which the salesperson leaves a 90-second message that we know *will never* be returned. What's worse? We just wasted someone's time, *and* wrote out a big fat check to our competitor. The client or prospect doesn't need to know the city you're in or what other number you've tried to reach them on. Who cares? The extra information in a message is actually a pollutant that's causing you to waste precious time! Simplify the message by stating only your name and number, and repeating your phone number. Most people will not catch it on their first time they hear it, but are likely to have a pencil and paper ready by the second time. Make it easy for people to return your call.

Here is an example of a primary message: "Greetings. This is Chuck calling long-distance for Sally Sue. *(Pause, silence, patience.)* Return my call at 123-456-7890. That's 123-456-7890." That's *all you need* in a primary message. Some of you would like to argue that "You're not leaving enough information for them to call you back." Though that's the gamble we take, I've found through observation, study, and the testimony of others that primary scripts less than 15 seconds long tend to garner some pretty effective results. For example, my student Heather learned of this keep-it-simple approach on a coaching call and implemented it the next day. Although she already had one of the best callback rates in her company, she called me two days later to report that she had *doubled* the number of callbacks she had been getting.

So keep it short, create curiosity, and omit any significant sales pitch or anything else that would give the person on the other end an excuse to *not* return your call. By leaving information out, you create another distinction that eradicates the perception that "this salesperson has nothing better to do."

Since it's possible—but not very likely—that you'll get a call back after just one message, let's now imagine that it's time to proceed to the secondary message. The call should not be longer than 30 seconds, and it should focus on your subject's pain points. This is where you reveal that you know about your client or prospect's pain or need, and that you can heal or fill it. A typical secondary message would begin with, "I can help you with your [pain or need]." Then stir up the pain and answer the question of why they should call you back—because, of course, you have the solution. Here is one sample secondary message: "Greetings, John. This is Chuck calling long distance from XYZ Company at 123-456-7890. *(Pause, silence, patience.)* I'm calling to offer you some significant solutions to your current situation and a plan of relief from [whatever pain it is]. Again, my number is 123-456-7890." Though you may reference their difficulty, you're making a positive statement by offering a solution—and that positive statement is more likely to elicit a return call.

It is appropriate here to leave a deadline, a call to action, or an important date if you wish. Just don't give them a specific time range, such as between 1 and 4 P.M.; some of my students make it harder for themselves and the client by trying to control the environment. Instead, we want to allow the client or prospect to return the call at their convenience. Never promise to call them back, because they will definitely ignore you when do you. The fact that you're even leaving a voicemail most likely means that they're already trying to ignore you.

Here are additional notes for leaving voicemail messages. If you know the person's first name, then use it—not "Sir," "Ma'am," "Mister," "Mrs.," or "Ms." Though you might believe otherwise, using their first name *is* professional. Also, do not leave website information, since it's a potential excuse for the prospect not to call you back. They may assume, "Oh, I don't need to call the salesperson back. I'll just go look at their website." This defeats the message's purpose: *to get a call back*. The website cannot close them on a sale. This is like having a fish on a hook and then cutting your own line. Your catch-of-the-day score? Zero.

Don't forget to control your rate of speech. Though you have only 15 to 30 seconds, you should not try to get in too much information or talk too quickly. This can get a little tricky here, because we want the person receiving our message to detect that *we are busy*. Remember the listenable pace—140 to 160 words per minute—and adjust your message proportionately. Also remember that silence in front of words can create connection. Remember P.S.P.—Pause, Silence, Patience—so that even on those 15-second or 30-second voicemails, you can use the power of silence before a particular word to draw your listener in.

The time of day that you call can also influence the likelihood of receiving a call back. The VIP happy hour is from 7 to 9 A.M., because this is when your competitors are not in their offices. Calling during these hours will distinguish you from others and, in many cases, you will be able to reach the client on this early-morning call—because you give the impression that you're extremely busy, and have time to make these calls only first thing in the morning. The second-best time frame for leaving messages is from 4 to 6 P.M. Again, most people who hear the phone ring during this time assume that it's likely to be someone who is as busy as they are, who didn't have time to call until this point in the day. Also, be aware of time-zone changes. I make sales calls in every time zone of the United States, and if you do the same, make sure to have a time-zone map in front of you to remain cognizant of happy-hour targets.

Tips for Effective Messages

- Keep them short and simple
- For a second message, have a compelling reason for the client to call back
- Eliminate titles before names
- Do not provide your website in message
- Control your rate of speech
- Plot your call time strategically

Let's address reality: you still might not have gotten a call back from the client you've been trying to reach despite leaving two messages. In fact, this will often be the case. Yet our goal is still the same—to get a call back. While you don't want to leave a third message, you don't want to drop your client either. You've got to stay in their consciousness by using T.O.M.A. tactics for them to remember you! So use this as an opportunity to do something different. Everyone reading this book has likely come across the "While You Were Out" pink slips used in nearly all offices on the planet. As mentioned in the Sales Tools chapter, use the *pink slip sales tactic* (see Figure 8.2).

Pink slip number 1, offered on my website (www.chuckbauer .com/pink), is an html version. When you open it, you select the entire object, copy it, and paste it into the body of your e-mail. Once pasted into your e-mail body, you can use the typing function to input your message. Now you can electronically pink slip 'em—a great way to stay in contact with someone or remind them that they owe you a phone call. Another thing you can do is to alter the html to omit the time stamp or customer's name; where it says "Date," you can type "Now," and where it says "Name," you can insert "VIP Client," and write a message that you can reuse in other e-mails. While you only have to make the message once, you can send it out numerous times without changing the content of the message.

Pink slip number two is a large $8\frac{1}{2}$-by-11-inch pink page that's simply a magnified "While You Were Out" slip. Just as with the html

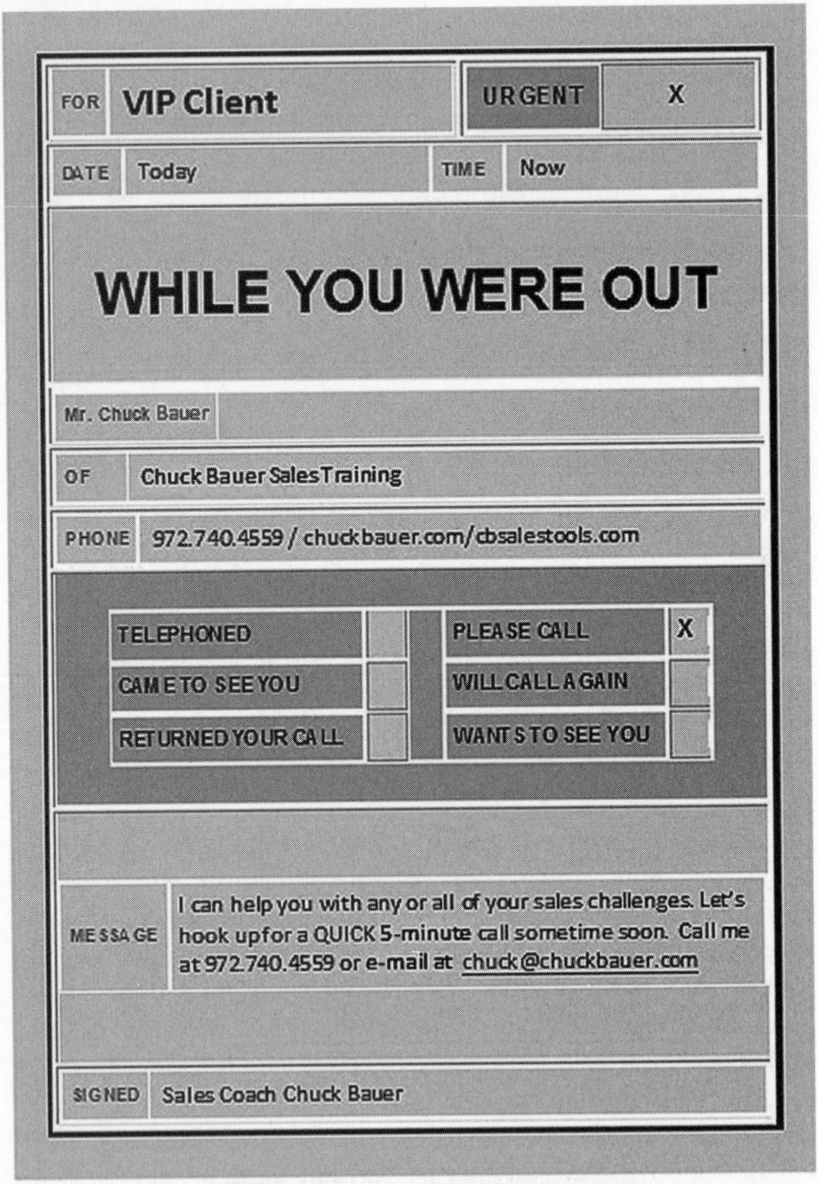

| FOR | **VIP Client** | | URGENT | X |

| DATE | Today | TIME | Now |

WHILE YOU WERE OUT

Mr. Chuck Bauer	
OF	Chuck Bauer Sales Training
PHONE	972.740.4559 / chuckbauer.com/cbsalestools.com

TELEPHONED		PLEASE CALL	X
CAME TO SEE YOU		WILL CALL AGAIN	
RETURNED YOUR CALL		WANTS TO SEE YOU	

| MESSAGE | I can help you with any or all of your sales challenges. Let's hook up for a QUICK 5-minute call sometime soon. Call me at 972.740.4559 or e-mail at chuck@chuckbauer.com |

| SIGNED | Sales Coach Chuck Bauer |

Pink Slip 'Em is freely distributed by Sales Coach Chuck Bauer.
Visit www.chuckbauer.com/pink or www.cbsalestools.com for more information.

www.chuckbauer.com • www.cbsalestools.com

FIGURE 8.2

version, you can take this one and propagate all the fields electronically, save it, and then send it to your clients so that when they receive it, it looks like a full bright page right on their computer. It makes for an attention-getting print-out, should their gatekeeper intercept it for delivery. The third pink slip file is an $8\frac{1}{2}$-by-11-inch version that prints out white so that you can write a message to a client and fax it or mail it. When was the last time you got a big-font fax saying that someone missed you? It's certainly an attention-getter.

Another follow-up course of action to elicit a client or prospect response is to go fishing (as in the Becoming a Sales S.T.U.D. chapter) twice a day in your daily work schedule—not for the same client, mind you. I've consulted for companies that have had some communication with a client that for whatever reason tends to drop off every once in awhile. This is when the company can choose one of the several fishing techniques. They can cast their communication lures into the pond of client orphans—once in the morning, and once in the afternoon. Across the country, we have a 20 to 40 percent success rate on the fishing techniques that we use and, let me tell you, that's a pretty awesome success rate compared to some of other methods you have tried. So use fishing techniques on the phone to make people call you back. You can also fish by cell phone. All you have to do is text "Call me right away" at the phone number. Just as with the other tactics, this will get your client's attention.

Finally, "the last resort" is a type of voicemail message used as a client termination tactic. Sounds harsh, doesn't it? Nobody wants to be terminated, of course, so when all else fails, you can politely threaten to close a client's file. Leaving that information in a voicemail may perhaps spark something in the person to make them want to call you back. You can make this statement a bit bolder and make it a direct hit to the jugular, or soften it somewhat—whichever you choose. A last-resort message might sound something like this: "John (*pause, silence, patience*), greetings from Scott at (corporate headquarters) here in Dallas. (*Pause, silence, patience.*) I'm calling in regards to closing your case file. I've been attempting to reach you for several weeks regarding your situation, yet I have not received a call back. Call me back and let me know if you would like me to close your file. 123-456-7890. Again, 123-456-7890." It's not a bad tactic—as long as it's used as a last resort.

Next Option after Two Messages
- Pink slip 'em (do something different!)
- Go fishing twice a day
- Leave a client termination message
- Use any of the T.O.M.A. tactics as expressed in the Marketing Yourself Shamelessly chapter

This next maneuver to achieve a call back is a very cool approach that comes from Kylie Vaughn, a sales-training manager with one of the big companies I work with in Dallas. She tags her messages at the end with "and I approve this message." I love that. It's different, it's distinctive, it's a little bit dorky, and a little bit political, but the fact of the matter is that it will get a chuckle and she will be remembered, in a way that someone with a more conventional sign-off would not be.

A lot of people ask me, "Should I even bother to leave a message?" In other words, are there times when it's preferable *not* to do so? There's no cookie-cutter answer to this question; it depends on your company, the direction of your management, as well as on a few other business profile factors. First of all, do you have a high or low volume of leads? What is the value of each lead? What is your company's policy regarding voicemails? What is the typical outcome of leaving messages versus not doing so? My personal preference in my own professional niche is to avoid leaving voicemails—period. However, that's me. You have to consider your own sales approach and company policy, and make the necessary adjustments.

Whether you attain a callback or not, what you do after the call will determine the strength of your echo. I believe that whenever you attain success on any of your calls, you need to follow up immediately. Don't forget to use the Outlook calendar "Invite" feature to schedule all future calls or tasks with your clients, as well as to attach documents that progressively layer into the sale. Let's say that you have concluded a call. You can attach any related documents in the Outlook calendar invite, along with the appointment for the next step, or you can use some of the fishing techniques from the Sales S.T.U.D. chapter. Approach all of your communications in a nontraditional way, whether you've already made a successful connection or are still fishing.

At the initial contact attempt and throughout your calling relationship with your prospect or client, you often talk to someone else first—the gatekeeper. You must treat gatekeepers with the highest levels of respect, for their daily responsibilities require that they sift through mounds of you-know-what every day. They receive calls five minutes before and after yours, so you must find a way to distinguish yourself with gatekeepers. The primary and secondary voicemail messaging systems work the same way with gatekeepers as with your clients themselves, with the exception that when you're speaking with a gatekeeper, you've got to make a strong claim about what your product, offering, or service can do for the owner of that company. Don't pitch them or get into details. Just make one clear assertion that they will remember—one in which you tell rather than ask. You can leave gatekeepers more than a couple of messages, but if you've left three or four and have not gotten a response, then stop. They are not going to return your call.

If the gatekeeper is a long-distance phone call and is with a VIP client you're attempting to reach, send that gatekeeper a gift—but do so *without* indicating who the gift is from. I usually mail or ship these gifts with no return address, which is possible through Priority Mail (U.S. Postal Service). Then I will refer to the gift the next time I call them, because they will have no clue where it came from, other than the postmark. Always give gatekeepers chocolate—it's an infallible attention-getter.

One oft-forgotten and underappreciated type of message is the outgoing, prerecorded voicemail greeting that you leave for people who call you. The details of this message should be treated with great care. You want to sound honest, enthusiastic, sincere, and as professional as possible. You do *not* want to sound bored, asleep, or angry. Yes, I've heard greeting messages that sound as if the person was taped while in a low-energy or emotional condition. As always, be mindful of body language, pitch, pace, and articulation. Remember P.D.R.—to practice, drill, and rehearse this message. Record, and then ask for feedback from your sales manager even if you feel you made no mistakes. Here's a sample of an outgoing voicemail message: "You've called the offices of XYZ Company. Last year, we (*state how you benefit clients*) and you could be the next _____ (*state an example of your solutions*)." Then, "Leave your name and number and I'll get back to you at the first available moment." Make sure you have a compelling reason for them to call you back.

The one sales action that deserves more respect than it gets is called cold calling. For those of you who have preconceived notions about cold calling, here's a story. I had a guy in a seminar a couple of years ago who told me "You know, people who cold call are the carp of the lake—the bottom dwellers." However, I know salespeople who make some pretty impressive incomes, and part of the reason they make those incomes is because they're cold calling. Cold calling is a part of their daily revenue-producing activities. They are not foolish enough to think of themselves as "bottom dwellers" and automatically take a 30 percent pay cut. It doesn't make sense. You've got to eradicate these kinds of false assumptions. Remember . . . find the reason *to* do it, not to avoid it! Yes, cold calling can be tough. And yes, people will hang up on you. They sometimes even say nasty things to you. But don't take it personally; just move on.

And believe it or not, you *can* make cold calling fun. You have to have a little bit of that sales edge—that smidge of an attitude that conveys to the person on the other end of the phone that you're not going to fall into great despair if they don't take your phone call or end up buying from you.

What you must remember about cold calling is that it's not about the calls you make; it's about the number of significant conversations that the calls bring forth. I hear statements all the time where salespeople brag, "I made 70 calls today," but you know what? The number of times you've dialed means nothing—not to your manager, your company's owner, or the board of directors. What *is* meaningful is the number of revenue-driving calls you produce. It's the same as when we talk about marketing yourself shamelessly: it's not counting the people you reach, but reaching the people who count.

To make any call efficient, you need a good headset. You should take electronic notes in either the CRM system you're using or in Outlook. If you don't have a headset, buy one or use your speakerphone if your office atmosphere is appropriate for it.

As it is with your other sales strategies, time is on your side—*if* it's scheduled properly! Cold calling requires the same kinds of time-management techniques as your other sales skills. Use the time block in Outlook early in the morning to do your cold calling; you shouldn't put this activity off until late afternoon, when you may well talk yourself out of it: "Oh, it's 3:00; I'll get my cold calling done at 3:15," and then you look up and it's 4:55, and then it's "Oh, I can go home. I don't need to do my cold calling today." Of course, if your company policy states that you have to do something in the late afternoon, that is understandable, but don't put cold calling off if you don't have to. Procrastination equals demotivation. If possible, isolate yourself completely when you make your calls. If you have an office, put a sign outside that reads "Do Not Enter." Don't let anybody disturb you. Get your cold calling done.

However, even with all of the best intentions, sales violations certainly happen in cold calling. The biggest one of these is that salespeople have a tendency to do *too much* research before making the call. They want to go to Google and look into the company's past performance. I call this "revenue aversion." I often run into salespeople who want to conduct ten minutes of research before they dial. No. Do not bother. It's a waste of time. Instead of trying to make everything perfect *before* the call, just concentrate on *making* the call—and then making it a perfect call.

If you've implemented the methods I've described up to this point, then you have already built up your skills through the tactics I've shared with you. Make sure your voice is not weak or monotone. Don't be timid or fearful. Engage the client, and eradicate their fears as quickly as possible. Make sure that you are listening to them. Don't talk over them. Discuss the product, service, or offering *with* them instead of pitching *to* them.

Once you are fully involved in a cold call, you have one main objective: to give a full presentation. There are then three possible routes to achieve this goal. The best possibility arises when you receive an opportunity to give a full presentation on that initial call, right then and there. The second avenue is to have that first call result in an appointment with that prospect or client for a full presentation in the very near future. And the third option is a call that occurs now as a fully intentional warm-up discussion that leads to a future full presentation. This simply means that if the client or prospect answers the call but only has a few minutes, you must engage them with a compelling reason to schedule a future appointment with you, and schedule it quickly.

At the conclusion of a cold call, ask for a referral. If you're on 10 or 15 significant calls every day and you ask for a referral for your specific company, product, offering, or service, chances are you're going to get at least a couple as a result of those attempts. All you have to do is ask, and always do so at the *end* of the call. Create the habit!

Remember when you do score on cold calls to use the same follow-up methods as with other client encounters. Put the person's information into Outlook. Send the Jim Rohn book of quotes to them. Prepare the mail pieces and staggered e-mail messages. Put them into the C.R.M. system if they've opted in. In other words, don't treat a successful cold call any differently from your other clients; follow up immediately.

Now, I have a request for sales managers. I have encountered, and gotten to know fairly well, some companies whose sales managers do not actively coach their salespeople on live phone calls, and some managers who give no coaching at all. My request is that you get out of your office and onto the floor and coach salespeople during their phone calls. This is how I do it: I mike up with a headset on and split into live calls. I'm right in front of the salesperson and I have a flip chart behind me (see Figure 8.3).

On the upper left-hand corner of the flip chart, I write the salesperson's name. Underneath their name is the word

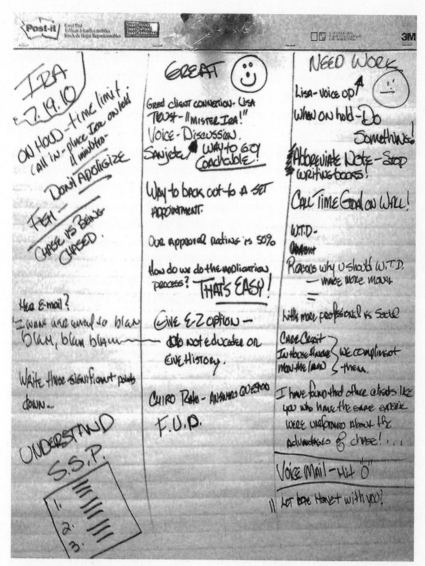

www.chuckbauer.com • www.cbsalestools.com

FIGURE 8.3

"Awesome," the middle column is labeled "Great," and the right-hand column is labeled "Needs work." Sometimes I'll use smiley faces, neutral faces, and frowny faces. As I'm listening in on a sales call, I jot down what they did well, things they missed, and areas in which they need to improve. Typically, if I'm on a 20-or-30-minute call, that flip chart will become completely covered with information.

Sales managers need to do the same thing. Relying solely on a recorded file discounts the value and influence of body language and environment. Some of the first items I record include whether the salesperson is standing when they make the phone call, if there is a mirror by the computer, the location of the salesperson's goals list, if they have pictures of their family on display, and the overall visual impressions of their surroundings that will keep them on "the hunt." I can surmise all of this in a mere five seconds. It tells me right away if this person knows what they're doing, or if more attention will be required to develop them as a salesperson.

So, a message to all you sales managers: "Get out there and get your hands dirty!" Don't sit back in your office and limit yourself and your team to listening to recorded calls. I know there are companies out there with sales managers who do not go live with their salespeople. If you are one of these managers, you don't understand the opportunities you are missing by not working shoulder-to-shoulder with your salespeople—the most direct way to help them get better and close more sales. Ignoring this opportunity is another type of revenue aversion to which you should not fall prey. Help your salespeople master their phone sales skills to cultivate higher earnings. It helps them, and it helps *you*.

To conclude, whether phone usage is only a fraction of your sales day or is the main event every hour, the phone as a tool should be more highly regarded as a portal to higher levels of sales success. Now that you understand the anatomy of a sales call, you can diagnose your own performance and make adjustments accordingly. Like anything else, you only get out of it what you put into it—so make it count.

Phone Mastery Commission Development Quiz

Anything fewer than 100 percent correct answers requires immediate additional work!

1. What personal item can increase your awareness of body language on a call when placed by the phone?

2. What are the three primary client fears to overcome in the first few seconds of a phone call?

3. How do you add horsepower to your voice for command?

4. True or False: It's more effective if you *tell* the client what to do instead of *ask*.

5. What quality do you express by addressing your own fears for a call?

6. What can you do to verify your sales qualities on the phone?

7. What is the goal of leaving a message?

8. For the most effective messages, which has been proven to produce a higher callback rate: information addition or information omission?

(continued)

(Continued)

9. What is the ideal length for primary and secondary messages?

10. True or False: It's more professional to precede the client's name with Mr., Ms., or Mrs.

11. True or False: It may increase your chances of a callback to mention your website.

12. What are the two times of the day that are best for V.I.P. happy hour calling?

13. True or False: If there is no response after two messages, keep calling. Don't give up.

14. What tool can you use to vary your communication attempts?

15. True or False: It's okay to terminate your client's file.

16. True or False: The T.O.M.A. campaign has little to do with phone sales.

17. True or False: In the big picture, voicemail greetings don't make an impact on the client.

(continued)

(Continued)

18. True or False: Cold calling does not need to be methodical.

19. True or False: It's best to find out as much as possible about your client before calling.

20. What is the main objective of a cold call?

21. What should you do at the end of a call?

Phone Mastery Quiz Answers

1. Mirror

2. You're selling, you're going to waste their time, and you're like all other salespeople

3. Stand up

4. True

5. Confidence

6. Record your calls and review them

7. To elicit a call back

8. Omission

9. 15 and 30 seconds

10. False

(continued)

(*Continued*)

11. False

12. 7 to 9 A.M. and 4 to 6 P.M.

13. False: Do something other than a call after a second un-returned phone call

14. Pink slip 'em

15. Absolutely true

16. False: It can actually solidify a phone sale and earn a referral

17. False: You still need to pay attention to the details

18. False: Time management still applies to cold calling

19. False: That's called revenue aversion. Make the call, then make it perfect

20. To give a presentation

21. Ask for a referral and do immediate follow-up

9

Overcoming Objections

Have you ever gotten a song stuck in your head? It plays over and over again in your mind, and then at your request, a good friend steps in to sing a new song to get the first one to stop. The same thing can happen in sales, when you begin hearing the same old objections time and again. Are you saying the same old thing in response to these objections, and getting the same old results? If you're overcoming the objections, that's a step in the right direction, but there are proactive ways to improve and facilitate the closing process for an even better outcome.

You should be keenly aware that utilizing traditional responses will yield traditional results. However, using *untraditional* responses at the right time is likely to get more gold into your pot at the end of the rainbow. There have been countless resources tackling the topic of handling objections over the years: some that are very accurate and still applicable in our current time, and some that are extremely outdated and no longer relevant in today's sales world. And although we've come to use the phrase "overcoming objections," there is so much more beyond the rebuttal in and of itself: sales psychology, the use of sales tools, specific tactics for specific objections, and so on. I have seen the struggles that occur when even highly skilled and veteran salespeople face the dreaded two-letter word "No." Whatever your level of expertise, you should know how to identify and work through a delayed decision. This chapter will be your ounce of prevention or your pound of cure, depending on how you use the information. So clear your throat, warm your whistler, and let's change the tune of those objections. (See Figure 9.1.)

FIGURE 9.1

The "first impression" principles you now know deserve some re-examination at this point. Making people *want* to do business with you is an ability you can control—one that addresses general objections before the prospect or client can bring them up. This skill is paramount, since clients buy *you* before purchasing your product, service, offer, or company. Do the hundreds of little things you do to make people want to do business with you actually work? Would your prospect remember *you*, even if he or she saw multiple sales-people in a day? Men, are you dressed to change the oil in your car, or do you have on nice slacks and a tie? Women, is your makeup neat and complete: foundation, powder, blush, eye shadow, eyeliner, mascara, lipstick? Without these in place, you look like a puzzle with a piece missing; however, don't wear too much either or you'll end up looking as if you work for the Ringling Brothers Circus. As a rule, earrings that brush the top of the shoulder look fine for evening or casual wear, but are a distraction otherwise. And don't wear those windshield-wiper eyelashes for the same reason. Keep perfume or cologne barely noticeable so that the person with whom you're meeting doesn't begin wishing for a gas mask. Bottom line: **our appearance should reinforce our professionalism, not detract from it.**

The processes you use will make your other distinctions evident to your client. You begin earning and justifying the right to get that person's business, even if your price is higher, by building intimacy with a client, exposing them to an established T.O.M.A campaign, and all the seemingly little but in fact big things that create familiarity. Have you remained in constant—yet not overbearing—communication with the client? While you want to stay in touch, you don't want to appear "needy;" therefore, your contact should be fairly *infrequent*, versus badgering the prospect five days a week with five voice messages or e-mails in a row. Too much contact takes away from the sale; you should stagger the communication, as we discussed in Chapter 2: Marketing Yourself Shamelessly. You don't want the client or prospect to hear your voicemail or see your e-mail and think "Ugh, him again!" and promptly hit the "delete" key.

Remember the Smokey the Bear campaigns from the 1980s, that lovable character who wanted us all to work together to prevent forest fires? As with large-scale disasters like forest fires, it's best to prevent objections before they even arise. So how do you do that? By anticipating what the objection could possibly be and then wrapping your presentation around that objection. As I already discussed when

I introduced you to the O.O.S. (Overcoming Objections Sheet) tool, this is likely to be based on the most common objections you hear in your field. A colleague of mine in Dallas works in the mortgage industry and hears four major objections more often than any others. Since he's so used to encountering these protests, he kills them before they ever come up by providing clients and prospects with four Overcoming Objection Sheets. You might have a standard presentation that you do for your prospects and clients, but if you can anticipate an oft-repeated objection, then you should work to design the presentation to address and invalidate that objection. Beat your client to the punch, so that he or she doesn't even have to mention the issue. How do I beat 'em? When I consult with companies about sales seminars, I've already been referred to them, so they already "know" me to some extent. But before I even meet with them, I've typically sent several pieces of literature (the *Treasury of Quotes* book, a couple of flyers), and they've visited my website, which is methodically designed to kill objections. So even though it's our first in-person encounter, our meeting already has sense of familiarity. And as they say—*that's* the beginning of a beautiful friendship.

When the first appointment arrives, I typically meet with the company CEO and executive vice president of sales. Had I not warmed up these company heads through my T.O.M.A. campaign, I would have a lot more work ahead of me, and would ultimately be forced to spend more time accomplishing the same goal. Setting up for this consultative conclave loosens their lips and entices them to share with me every element of their needs and challenges relating to their sales force. I use this intelligence to identify and strategize the artillery that I'll need to guarantee the sale.

After the meeting, I'll usually walk the sales floor, look around, speak to some of the salespeople, and continue to gather data. Then the heads and I reconvene in the conference room and I tell them, "First of all, I'm honored that I've been asked to take a look at your company to see if I can offer you a solution. The solution I'll construct to meet your needs will be made through a formal presentation that I will hand-deliver to you in a timeline of between seven and fourteen days." When I'm here in Dallas, I always present this information face-to-face, and make an effort to do so in most places in the United States, if the project is big enough. I then inform the company leaders that I will schedule a time in seven days for all of us to sit down and review the proposal together. Notice that I'm talking about deadlines here—and that I'm telling, not asking.

I then look them squarely in the eyes and say "The investment that you make in the price that it's going to take for you to get my solution will be my very best price. With respect, I don't negotiate. That's my policy, because that price I give you *is* my best price. I don't accept payments on the investment. I allocate time, resources, and my team for any major or minor need on the project, so I expect full payment. Everything must be paid in advance. In addition to that, I promise you that if you go out and meet with other sales coaches or other sales trainers, that I will be the most expensive. If you're just buying based on price and not looking for a return, not seeking a long-term solution, or not looking for the latest and greatest information about the sales industry, then I'm not your guy. You have to go to those smaller training companies, because I'm going to be more expensive. However, the last thing I want to share with you is that I will deliver the *highest value* for your company. I will do whatever it takes with your company; I don't care how big the sales force is. I can guarantee this, because I do it with so many other companies. I know I'm going to accomplish the goal and meet the objective."

Yes, I *do* say all of these things. And I mean every word. My first price *will be* my best price. I *don't* negotiate. I *don't* take payments. I *will* be the most expensive. And I *will* deliver the highest value to my clients. I'm very confident about this, because I've done it before. Because I convey this confidence through my words, tone, and body language, objections don't ever come up. When I go back and deliver the solution to my clients, I get a "Yes," a yes with some small changes, usually involving scheduling or a tweak in the method, or a "No." There's no reason for your approach to be any different. Kill any potential objections so that they don't come up at all. Work smarter—not harder.

Another way to thwart objections is to sell and respond to a client's particular personality style. If you don't understand personality selling, then you are apt to be closing people in the way that *you* want to be closed, and not necessarily what they prefer—something that may result in not closing them at all. For example, when a thinker tells you, "I need to think about it," they're making a truthful statement. If a director, socializer, or relater claims that they need to think about something, however, it's usually a smoke-screen phrase meant to conceal the other reasons why they are not going forward with the offer.

There's one very powerful word you can use when encountering objections: *why*. Think of it this way: if an ego-based client is giving you pushback, the word *why* will help you to determine the root of the sales interruption and allow you to resume the conversation's forward momentum. You might consider asking the ego-based person, "May I ask you why you're thinking that way?" And then be quiet. Let them vent and get everything out at that point.

You can ask the same way if a feelings-based person is pushing back; however, you should use the word *feel* instead of *think*: "May I ask you why you're feeling that way?" You also want to acknowledge their point of view: "Your position is interesting, and I respect what you're saying, but I need to ask why you *feel* that way?"

Regardless of the intensity or duration of the client's answer, once again, let them vent. In many cases, the client may realize that he or she is on the wrong side of the debate, thus allowing them to talk themselves out of their own objection. Let them express their frustrations, listen to them, and have a discussion in which you are both engaged. At the end of your discussion, make sure to isolate the issues once again, to make sure there's nothing else that might prevent you from closing that deal.

Another tactic in smoothing the sale is to realize that people don't want to be sold; however, they *do* want to feel like they're buying. Refer to your notes on the qualities and habits of feelings-based and ego-based personality types, because they will manifest themselves *everywhere*. Feelings-based people will openly share their feelings with you right then and there, while ego-based people will look around, make sure no one is looking at them, and *then* check with their feelings and make sure they want to buy what it is that you're selling. You can foster the sense that they are *buying* a product instead of having it sold to them by having in-depth, quality discussions with your clients and prospects. Forget using the guerrilla sales tactics from back in the 1970s; those simply do not work nowadays. So stuff those old antics back into your metal lunchbox and keep them there.

You can also prevent the big "N-O" by delivering strong presentations with irrefutable evidence. Let's review your Sales Mastery checklist to remember how your sales tools can battle objections. First, you should have instituted an effective T.O.M.A. campaign (Chapter 2) to actively and preemptively **address and prevent objections**. The next step is to establish yourself on the C.B.S.—the Client's Believability Scale (see Figure 7.1). You want to perform in the green zone, where you pitch, use visual effects and third party stories or examples, and get the client involved. At that point, you should have a one-page sales sheet prepared that is designed to quash any objection. You should also have client audio files (MP3s) of past presentations you've given in which you were required to overcome an objection and your efforts resulted in a sale. You can also email these audio files to your clients as part of your T.O.M.A. campaign. Have them ready on your iPad or other device during future presentations, so that you can listen to the audio when you're with a client.

While we're on the tech wavelength, don't forget to utilize the video file in the same function as the audio file. Don't be shy—record your sales successes! Let's say you have a client who is going to buy your product and you manage to overcome any protests they've made. The client ends up purchasing the product, and is completely satisfied with it. Take the opportunity to record this person on videotape right then and there. Any audios and videos you make should be no longer than 60 seconds, and should show your customer giving testimony that is something like the following: "I considered buying this product, but I had an issue with X. My salesperson helped me understand the issue, and I went ahead and bought the product.

Now, I am satisfied." Constantly increase your arsenal of third party stories, and don't be afraid to pull out the big guns, like

- An effective T.O.M.A. campaign
- C.B.S.—Client Believability Scale
- One Page Sales Sheets
- Client Audio and Video Files

So let's address reality: usually, it's when you have to verbally overcome objections that your wit and sales skills are *really* put to the test. My students frequently call or e-mail me with objections, and I end up asking them questions to review a vital point: "Who is selling whom? Are you buying into the objections yourself? In that case, then, aren't *you* the one who's really being outsold by your client? Maybe *my* clients' companies should hire *your* prospects for a sales position, instead of you." In many cases, that is exactly what's happening. I recommend that my students acknowledge a prospect's objection and then move on as if to ignore it, because most of these objections are not even valid. In the rare instance that you aren't able to prevent an objection that surfaces from Lake Nowhere, you want to drown it right away. Then you can take another breath and move on to closing the transaction.

I've read several sales books that state that while the objection means "No" for now, it doesn't necessarily equal "No" down the road. Or, a "No" means that more information is needed. Here's what it boils down to: *any* opposition you hear is a red flag telling you that the client needs motivation, and there are only two ways to motivate someone else. The first is to appeal to their desire for gain or pleasure. The second is to eliminate a fear of loss or pain. Frankly, if you've been listening to your client, you will be able to quickly identify the direction in which your conversation needs to move.

You can isolate any objection that arises through honest communication with the client, while consulting thoroughly to be sure you're not about to swallow a fishbone. Find out if it is a true objection or just a smokescreen to another problem, concern, or past negative experience.

Then, reestablish the client or prospect's focus on the product, offering, or service's specific features and distinction. Reemphasize its benefits through open dialogue and exchange, rather than just purely pitching. I often like to ask prospects or clients to tell me what particular point *they* remember about the offering. Continue to build the value of your offering, service, or product by consistently engaging them.

Any objection you hear is likely to fit into one of five explanatory categories. The first is that **you have not established a need** for your prospect. If you find that their doubts fall under this category, simply review your presentation, identify the challenge, state a resolution for it, and reestablish the need.

The second category is some form of the claim that your client or prospect **"doesn't have the money."** Your first job is to reemphasize the need for them to somehow *find* the money, while simultaneously acknowledging that everybody does have the resources if they need or want something badly enough. I always try to build my presentations in such a way that makes potential clients want my product so much that they'll figure out a way to get the coin. It's just that simple. Again, do I get every one of them? No. But when they say "I don't have the money," I know that 9 times out of 10, they *do*. I can't tell you how many times a year I hear companies say, "We don't have the budget for it," only to have the funds magically appear three months later. That's because I've ignored their lack-of-funds excuse, determined their needs and challenges, introduced a solution, given them an investment price, and—what do you know?—I get the sale. Salespeople who hear "I don't have the money" and respond by saying "Well, that's okay," are folding like a lawn chair. That approach is never going to work.

To further the conviction that price objections don't come up as often as you may think they do, let's discuss the "self-fulfilling prophecy." The first thing to confront is your attitude. I've become acquainted with salespeople who, for whatever reason, always seem to be broke. They've had some issues, and the economy has hit their families pretty hard. I have complete empathy for these people, and I truly want their situations to improve. However, I've also found that if they're broke, they frequently assume that the rest of the world is broke too. To that end, these salespeople are the ones who typically come up with more price objections than anyone else—even more than the clients. If you are a salesperson or a manager of salespeople who doesn't believe strongly enough in your product, then prospects are going to have a hard time believing in that product as well, because you're emitting a degree of doubt that other people can sense. You have to really pay attention to your outlook and check your own attitude if you get that price objection. If you have a great attitude, chances are that a price objection won't hit as hard as it would if you have a less positive one.

Another attitude adjustment that will help you overcome price objections is to be *enthusiastic*. Don't be too heavy-handed with logic and product knowledge; surveys have already told us that prospects and clients want *enthusiastic* salespeople. I'm not talking about doing Red Bull–induced back flips in your client's office; I'm just talking about having a great level of energy and passion. Smile, and remember to use positive body language; you're better off smiling quietly than talking ad nauseum in monotone.

The third category into which client objections fit is **a lack of urgency**. If your prospects don't feel an incentive to move quickly, it's typically because you haven't motivated them—whether through the green zone in the C.B.S. or via the S.T.U.D. method: Specific Next Steps, Takeaway, Urgency, and Deadline. Ask yourself "What am I not doing?" How can I institute a sense of urgency into this sales process? Failing to establish a deadline is one of the most common and detrimental mistakes in sales. Even students who have been to one or more of my seminars will be shy or nervous to take this approach. They'll tell me "Oh, Chuck, I'm not sure about putting a deadline on a person." Sometimes this fear has to do with the language you use. If you need to step it up a notch, then make your language bolder. You can soften it somewhat if you're a little nervous about it, but do make sure to establish deadlines. And remember to always use the Outlook calendar feature when setting these targets. I work with banks, giant corporations, and multimillion dollar institutions all the time and guess what? I put deadlines on them! It works. These people and companies realize we're all professionals. It's no big deal.

The fourth category of potential protests is a **lack of client confidence**. If the client or prospect doesn't have confidence in you and the sales progress seems frozen, it's because they have unresolved Fear, Uncertainty, and Doubt that you haven't managed to quell. You can remedy this impediment through great presentations, by figuring how the client relates to others, using sales tools, and including Overcoming Objections sheets. It also benefits your confidence to fill your pipeline, because this will give you a little bit of that sales edge attitude that conveys "I really don't care if you do this with me, 'cause I got a gazillion other things going on over here this week!" It makes *them* chase *you*—not the other way around. So exude confidence to remove the F.U.D. fortress that's blocking your sale.

The fifth category for common sales debacles is failing **to have all decision makers present at the time of sale**. The classic scenario is the husband/wife objection—and the real go-getters out there push for the sale, even if only one decision-maker is present. Pitching to the husband or wife in the absence of the other is a "one-legged call"—because although you might think your power of persuasion will excite him or her enough to go home and convince their spouse, to buy from you . . . well, you're wrong. Think about it: whoever attempts to do the convincing isn't going to know how to pitch the product like you do. And you're not just getting a "No;" you're getting one that's been dragged through the mud. The husband who is then pitched by his wife hours after your presentation will make comments like, "I've got this other person who does this," or "Let me check with my friends, relatives, coworkers, and on Google." When you let someone make your pitch for you, I guarantee you will lose the sale 9 times out of 10. So why are you pitching a one-legged call? It doesn't make sense, and it wastes both your and your clients' time. What is the lesson here? You always want to arrange the situation favorably by getting all decision-makers together before you pitch to avoid sabotaging yourself.

For review, here are the five main objection troubleshooting categories.

1. **No need.** In these cases, review the presentation and adapt to the challenge. *Make it* a need.

2. **No money.** Reestablish the importance of attaining the product/service so that the client is able to "find" room in their budget.

3. **No urgency.** Make it clear that this need should be fulfilled as soon as possible. Motivate clients with third party stories, testimonials, and use deadlines.

4. **No confidence.** Kill any remaining F.U.D. and then confidence will replace fear.

5. **Not all decision-makers present.** Some examples are husband/wife, two store owners/managers, or an entire corporate team. Make sure everyone's there, or you're setting yourself up for failure.

Perhaps, however, you haven't even *gotten* an objection yet. The time lapse between the point of ending your sales talk with a client and the point of a client's final "Yes" or "No" decision is referred to as being in "sales jeopardy." This shouldn't simply be a waiting period for you; rather, you've got to do *something*! Some salespeople simply opt to watch grass grow while they're in sales jeopardy. By doing so, they're running the risk of losing a sale. Remember this: a delayed decision leaves more room for "No." While this doesn't mean that you'll end up getting a refusal from a prospect or client every time you experience a delay, you don't want to be lazy and simply let things happen. If that's your attitude, it's time for a career reconsideration.

Here are some actual comments that my sales students have made to me when they've been delayed for one reason or another.

- "I know for sure I've got the sale."
- "They told me I will get their business."

- "He reminds me of my grandpa. I am so sure I am getting this deal."

- "I am 100 percent sure that they will buy from me."

- "I am buying you a steak dinner and a bottle of wine when the money comes in."

These reactions are sure signs of self-deception. While it's evident that everybody *hopes* they'll make the sale, you're in trouble if you're hoping all the time. You're either the salesperson who *isn't* hoping (because you're closing business), or the one who is routinely wishing, guessing, and hoping that the sale is "somehow" going to come in. But hoping won't close sales; only action will.

The "hope" mentality can actually be dangerous in the sales profession. Think about it this way: you're a pilot flying along and you hear the engine make a little chitty-chitty-bang-bang noise. You look down at the instruments and they're off just a little bit, so you begin hoping at this point that the engine doesn't quit. But in some cases, the engine *does* quit, and now you're up in the air having to land without an engine. Or you look down and see that the gas gauge is fluctuating, even though you thought the plane had more gas when you took off than it evidently does. But you're hoping that there will somehow be enough gas in the tank to get you where you're going. These are pilots who, unfortunately, are not going to make it to their final destination. Hope in sales is (almost) as disastrous as it is in aviation. So you have to learn not to rely on hope and, instead, **take action to close business.**

Sometimes you *don't* overcome the objections, and you *do* lose the deal. When that happens, get over it and move on. It's okay to get upset for a couple of minutes, but after that, get back to selling. And always send a thank you after a "No!" Here is a simple script that you can use when this happens: "It is with sincere regret that your immediate plans do not include committing to _____. However, I appreciate your time and consideration. If you need further information, please feel free to call on me. In addition, I will keep you posted on further developments with _____." Dwelling on the lost sale wastes your time and energy, and sometimes the time and energy of others as well. There was a financial planner in a

MasterMind group of seven people who met through a conference call three times a month who spent seven minutes of this call complaining about a deal he had just lost. Considering there were seven people on the call, spending seven minutes in this kind of negativity was essentially wasting 49 minutes of time—almost an entire hour. When this man finished his tirade, I asked one of my students on the call to tell us what the actual issue was. He explained, "The real reason you're upset is because your pipeline's not full, because if your pipeline was full, you would have never spent seven minutes talking about how you just lost this deal." And that's the truth. When you have a lot of other potential clients, you might get upset, but it's only going to be for a couple of seconds. You're not going to go vent to a sales buddy or online because you simply don't have time; you're too busy selling to all the other people. And remember: it's not always realistic to expect a 100 percent closing rate. I'm pretty dang good, and even I don't close every one of my deals—and neither will you. **When a sale doesn't happen, put it behind you, and move on.**

But wait! There's also the "No" in the cases when people may be bluffing you, or asking for a lower price as a means to making it a game for them. For example, any time I buy *anything*, I always ask **"Is that the best you can do?"** I was once working with a car insurance agent named Pam who had attended a seminar of mine. Afterwards, I approached her and asked "Pam, would you send me a quote on my GMC Denali?" and she replied "Sure, Chuck, I'll send it to you." She proceeded to send me this very elaborate car insurance proposal. I looked it over and was able to ascertain that the price was a fair offering; certainly it was within the ballpark of what I had expected to pay. However, despite this realization, I sent her an e-mail and asked: "Is that the best you can do?" And that's *all I asked*. Within five minutes, that insurance rate went from about $850 a year down to something like $520. That price drop couldn't have been more instant if you had added water and stirred!

Now if Pam had written back "That is my best price, Chuck," I would have e-mailed her back "Okay. Done. Not a problem." So let that be a lesson, salespeople: when someone asks if you can go any lower—*just say no*. Then be quiet and see what happens. That doesn't mean that you should *never* reduce your price to get a deal;

we do that every day. But say "No" first, and wait for a response. Who knows? You might end up increasing your gross income. You might retain higher commissions (wink). You might have just given yourself a raise!

Another reason you may get an objection on price is because your prospect or client has seen a lower price elsewhere. When that happens, isolate the objection by agreeing that this competition does exists and acknowledging that this other price may indeed be lower. Then, confidently express to them that they will get more value for their money if they do business with you. Explain that whoever is offering that lower price could actually be offering something that will have less value to them in the long run.

Let's go into a deeper discussion about what happens when people say "No." The prospect's thought process is, "Can you give me a better price? Can you lower the amount? Can you do something better?" Most sales people's brains then endure synaptic breakdown as they hem and haw about it. As I stated earlier, **you have to say "No."** You snip the cord of their thought process with this two-letter word immediately and confidently—and then be quiet and observe their reaction to see if they're going to go ahead and pay for it or not. This approach won't squash the deal; it will simply interrupt their thought process. Make the client's thought of a better price retreat back into his or her brain. You don't need to say "Well, okay, maybe . . . let me go talk to my boss." No! Don't fold like the lawn chair. Be decisive when you say no. As soon as you do, it's a P.S.P. situation: Pause, Silence, and Patience. Some of my sales students have dubbed this the "shock and awe treatment;" people are shocked when you say no, because they're never heard "No"! The rest of the bruised and bloodied sales world says "Yes, I can give you a better deal." So stop doing that. Take a different—and more profitable—approach.

After you have said no and enacted P.S.P. and still haven't received a response from the client, you might say something like "And here is why I cannot reduce the price, because we believe that we have offered you a fair price—one that gives you a fair deal and one that makes us a small profit. It's a win-win for both of us. Our company is in the business of providing XXX (then mention three major benefits and continue); we're not in the business of making ill-conceived professional decisions. The price is what it is, and we both know that it is beneficial to both of us. Based on that, shall we proceed with the order?" It's that easy.

Know this and know it loud and clear: when you reduce your price immediately at their suggestion, you just *devalued* yourself, your company, and your product! It is okay to negotiate; just do it at the right time, after the right chain of events has occurred as I have described here. Ninety-five percent of all price negotiations are done at the wrong time and in the wrong way!

Support your presentation, claims, and pricing all the way up until the close, and always perform with sales integrity. Whether you're trying to overcome a price or any other kind of objection, be very careful not to come off as "sales-y" during negotiations. I have reviewed countless transcripts and audio files from many companies in which closes have deteriorated, and I find it so funny to hear salespeople hold onto a price while preaching value. Then when the price gets booed by the client, the salesperson caves and reduces it! Stop doing that. It doesn't make sense. You've worked hard to build up this great pitch, presentation, discussion about how wonderful your product, offering, or service is—only to abruptly diminish it by reducing the price.

For example—the following is an exact transcript from a recorded call.

Prospect: . . . and this whole package would add up to . . . ?

Salesperson: I'm almost there—hang in there! You also get a lifetime membership to the helpline. The *regular* price is $6,500; however, since these are tough economic times for everybody, I can work with you on that price.

Prospect: Yeaaah . . . (laughing)

Salesperson: I'll be honest, I have a lot of room to work with you on the price. As well as some added value.

Violation #1: The prospect asks a direct price question and the salesperson avoids an immediate answer. All is lost at this point.

Violation #2: "Hang in there?" Why, because your script is way too long and you know it? You shouldn't make the client feel as though they have to *endure* a conversation with you.

Violation #3: "The price is $6,500; *however* . . ." After the word "however" the client is smart enough to raise his own bulls—t flag!

Violation #4: "I'll be honest. . . ." What does that mean—that you *haven't* been up to this point?

This type of language has a negative impact on other salespeople as well, by supporting the unsavory reputation to which the field of sales routinely falls prey. You should know what *not* to say—and then *don't say it*!

Another way to develop your skills in overcoming objections is to perform this exercise in your offices. Sales managers can do it with your salespeople, and salespeople can do it with each other. Practice it diligently, and really put some effort into it. First, write out a potential objection. Then brainstorm by asking yourself, "By using my presentation and the Sales Mastery lessons I've learned from Sales Coach Chuck's book, how can I prevent the objection from occurring in the first place?" Then write it out in as much detail as possible. Don't be brief; brevity here means a lack of commitment. Think about what you can do differently, and record all of your ideas in detail. You never know what you'll come up with when you start brainstorming on paper. Comprehensively cover every angle of prevention, and then go on to the next thing, and to the next thing, until your metamorphosis is complete.

When figuring out how to prevent or eliminate an objection—whether in practice with colleagues or thinking on paper—decide what tools you are going to use, and consider what you can change in your presentation. Do you need a one-page Overcoming Objections Sheet to conquer client protests? Do you have an audio file for the prospect or client to listen to so they can hear how you do so? Though many salespeople already have brochures and other hard copy sales tools meant to overcome objections, there's a problem with this: if I were to walk into your office with a white glove and run my finger across the top of those brochures and sales tools, I would probably find dust on them. Get it? Dusty marketing tools aren't just keeping your feather duster unemployed; they're symbols of neglect and inactivity that have become a hindrance to your ability to trounce objections and close deals. This may even be symptomatic of a case of revenue aversion or laziness with which you have stricken yourself—and of which you may not be aware.

Devise additional tools of distinction to deal with habitual client complaints. Do you have 60-second audio or video files of a live client that you could use as a short, sweet commercial to surgically strike objections? After all, who are they going to believe more—you (the person selling the product) or another satisfied client? The client, of course, so use that confirmation to your advantage, and to close more sales.

Last but not least: if you are going to give something up—by lowering the price or making other efforts to please the client—then you *must* get something back. This could be as easy as receiving a guarantee for a full-fledged, 100 percent bona fide referral. I ask for a name, complete address, phone number, date of birth, hobbies or passions, and any other relevant information that I can use to prepare for a sales call. I'll also tell my current client, "If I'm going to give you a price break here, can we make a phone call to this person together so that you can introduce me to him?" Some people want a referral to be kept in confidence. That's okay; I'll do that. I still have the opportunity to use that contact information. Let me repeat: do not, under any circumstance, *ever* give anything up unless you can get something of significance back from that person. For me, it's as easy as getting a referral or two; it might be something else for you. But make sure you get something from that client, thereby ensuring a win-win situation. (See Figure 9.2.)

It's not about

luck!

We take the guessing out of your sales processes, and turn time into money!

www.chuckbauer.com • www.cbsalestools.com

FIGURE 9.2

Discipline, tenacity, and implementation inspire the following verse.

Objecting to Objections

Gain versus loss, pain versus pleasure,

This is the tune in its second measure.

"No" from the client, and "No" from you—

Can you answer the question of who's selling who?

Confidence is winning, and hope is disaster.

Are you working hard to be a Sales Master?

You must prevent, and yet overcome;

And if you cannot, it doesn't mean that you're done.

The "No" could be bluffing, so you must reconsider;

Recompose yourself and don't be a quitter.

"Overcoming Objections" Commission Development Quiz

Anything fewer than 100 percent correct answers requires immediate additional work!

1. Traditional responses will yield _____ results.

2. We should remember that our appearance should reinforce our professionalism, not _____ from it.

(Continued)

3. _____ kills F.U.D. and can be used in preventing and overcoming objections.

4. One of the most powerful words for discovering the basis of the client's objection is "_____."

5. _____ are extremely effective for strengthening a presentation and for battling objections.

6. Some objections given aren't valid, thus it's best to give a simple acknowledgment, then _____ it and move on.

7. When a prospect claims to not have the money, and the salesperson sheepishly says "That's okay," this is called _____ like a _____ _____.

8. The most influential and potent attitude adjustment is to be _____.

9. A lack of urgency from the prospect to make a decision would be created if the salesperson didn't perform in the green zone of the _____ or if he or she hadn't used the _____ plan of action.

(continued)

(*Continued*)

10. The lapse in time between the point of ending your sales talk with a client and the point of a client's final "Yes" or "No" decision is referred to as being in _____.

11. Instead of relying on hope, take _____ to close business.

12. When someone asks you for a discount, you should say _____.

13. It's called the "shock and awe" treatment because the rest of the sales world says "_____."

14. After practicing P.S.P., a good follow-up dialogue might be like this: "And here is why I _____ reduce the price. We believe we have offered you a _____ price, one that gives you a _____ deal and one that makes us a small _____. It's a _____-_____ for both of us. Our company is in the business of providing (give three main benefits and continue). We're not in the business of making _____ business _____. The price is what it is and we both know that this is a _____-_____. Based on that, shall we _____ with the _____?"

(*continued*)

(*Continued*)

15. When asking for a referral, you should ask for what six things?

16. True or False: If you give something up to the client and get nothing back from them, it's okay.

Overcoming Objections Quiz Answers

1. Traditional

2. Detract

3. Confidence

4. Why

5. Sales tools

6. Ignore

7. Folding, lawn chair

8. Enthusiastic

9. C.B.S. (Client's Believability Scale), S.T.U.D. (Specific Next Steps, Takeaway, Urgency, and Deadline)

10. Sales jeopardy

11. Action

12. No

(*continued*)

(Continued)

13. Yes

14. Cannot, fair, fair, profit, win-win, inappropriate, decisions, win-win, proceed, order

15. Name, complete address, phone number, date of birth, their hobby or passion, and any other information that could be helpful in preparing for the call.

16. False

10

Closing Mastery

Everything I've taught you thus far will be completely for naught if we don't close your business. Out of all the steps of a sales process, closing is as easy as hunting for sand on the beach. In fact, this chapter should consist of only one sentence: *Ask for the sale.*

If you are a F.O.N. (Freak of Nature) in sales, then your chapter on closing was the one *before* this one. It's likely that you've already executed each chapter as you read them, and all that remains is simply to answer the client's question as to which credit cards you accept. If that's the case, then *mazel tov!*

However, if it *hasn't* been that simple for you—which I am assuming is the case, since you're still reading—I have been purposeful throughout this book in emphasizing how critical it is that you've done the prior exercises for the next step to work. You can't expect to close the client if you didn't set up the sale. You must *earn* their business and perform all the prerequisites necessary. If you *are* finding it difficult to close them, then chances are that you've left something out. Losing the sale is a symptom of something that went wrong with *you*: making a false assumption like "He's dressed like a bum; he can't be a serious client," being lazy and thinking "I'll follow up later," or making an excuse such as "His listening skills are terrible: he doesn't even look me in the eye and then he interrupts when I speak." If the close isn't easy, then take responsibility and fix it. The close will only be as difficult as *you* make it.

The paradox with closing is that it actually starts at the *beginning* of the sales process. It begins with the way that you deliver the first 10 words out of your mouth at the initial contact—whether those words are written or spoken, over the phone or in person. The primary communication is what truly builds the foundation for a lifelong relationship with all of your clients.

So are you creating an unforgettable positive first impression? We always remember first place, but we usually don't remember second place. Case in point: who was the first person to fly solo across the Atlantic Ocean? Charles Lindbergh. We all know that. But who was the second? Do you remember that? We all know that Neil Armstrong was the first man to walk on the moon, but do you know who the second one was? Do we ever remember or bother to talk about the person who came in second? We don't. The same holds true in sales: you have only one chance to make a positive *first* impression. And if it's not positive, it's negative; there's no in-between. I am approached on a weekly basis to solve sales challenges, and I have found that before I begin to delve into a solution, I typically have to shift gears to reverse and fix something that occurred during the "first impression" stage before going forward. It happens all the time. If you fumble your first impression, you're going to have a lot of trouble with the rest of the process.

Your distinguishing habits and qualities are other major facets of your ability to close. **What distinguishes you from other people?** Remember: your personal and professional distinctions affect each other. Don't assume that your non-career-based characteristics and actions won't bleed into your professional life. Everything is intertwined.

I've heard sales managers say, "Leave your personal problems outside when you come into the office, and leave your professional challenges here when you go home." Guess what? That doesn't work! Feelings are a constant wave—sometimes a mere ripple, and sometimes a tidal wave. But whatever their magnitude, they are a part of who we are, 24/7. And although we can *manage* our feelings, we can't turn them off.

So since your personal distinctions are an undercurrent to your professional ones, ask yourself the following questions.

- Are you taking good care of yourself?
- Do you look and act sharp?
- Are you attentive?
- Do you listen, or do you think about lunchtime or what you're going to do after work?

Again, your professional and personal lives are absolutely connected. It is *your* responsibility, and yours alone, to achieve accomplishments in your personal life. Health has a direct impact on your entire existence, so start eating better. *Stop* eating at fast food restaurants and *start* choosing foods that are conducive to high energy, healthy appearance, and physical well-being, and thus create a more positive impression in your clients' minds. This is all that it takes to make them *want* to do business with you.

The next thing to ask yourself is: what are some of your *professional* distinctions?

- Do you market yourself like every other salesperson out there (or do you market yourself at all)?
- Do you use the same procedures and closings? Or do you do things differently and therefore more effectively?
- Did you send immediate follow-up messages to potential clients after the first point of contact?
- Are you using sales tools, audio files, and video files?

These qualities are what make people want to do business with you—*if* you are doing the right things.

You can also distinguish yourself as a professional persuader by being transparent and truthful with your words and feelings. Why do you have such conviction in your product or service? What is your opinion of your company? What are your feelings about yourself? Are you radiating confidence, which will encourage clients to believe in you? Feelings equate to truth, and the client or prospect can tell when you are speaking from the heart, especially since your heart is connected to your brain. Prospects will detect the truth and make a decision based on *you*! **A positive disposition** will lead to a **positive buying decision.**

Once you have earned a closing conversation with someone, here are some basic statements to tie them down and guide them toward a conclusive yes:

- It's a powerful solution, isn't it?
- Sounds like a plan that makes sense, correct?
- So far, so good?
- Sounds reasonable?
- This is what you want, correct?
- You think/feel the same way?
- Isn't that right?
- Is there any part of this you don't understand?
- Does this help?
- Don't you agree?

Another way to fan the flames and facilitate a close is to build consensus. Since we want to be on the same page as the prospect or client, then G.A.R.A. (Grateful, Appreciate, Respect, Agree) is your magic acronym to ease your client into an agreement. These four words are best used when overcoming objections, in times of conflict (or preventing conflict), and during your closing. Using them will keep everybody on the same page. For example, you might say, "I am **grateful** for the information you've just shared with me," "I

appreciate your position on the product that we're talking about," "I **respect** your position and where you are right now," or "I fully **agree** with your comment." Those are four easy examples of how to use G.A.R.A. to build the consensus you need to close the deal. You should also have the previously mentioned chorus line ready to go in your everyday sales toolbox. The minimum number of lines that I require my students to memorize is two: one strictly for feelings-based people, and one strictly for logic-and-ego-based people. Chorus lines don't need to be lengthy: 15 words or so will do. But don't forget that they should always begin with the words "Based on" and then finish with "Based on what I've just shown you," "Based on the numbers," "Based on the payment" Use your chorus lines as part of an effective closing.

If you dissect different types of tactics and closings, you will find that there are more complicated closings than the chorus line. But I must warn you: these closes aren't fireproof. While they *do* work in specific situations, you need to develop high levels of sales maturity and discernment to incorporate them into your sales process. If they aren't used at the right time or in the right situation, they'll backfire.

The eight closing choices that you have, besides your chorus line, are the following.

1. The test
2. The choice
3. The delayed decision
4. The assumptive
5. The cushion
6. The smoke-out
7. Third party stories
8. Feel/felt/found

Let's look at each one in more detail.

Test closes are exactly what they sound like: a test to find out exactly where our prospects are in their thought processes. Are they on the fence, or moving closer? Do we need to back up and cover something else? The test close is designed to uncover what the prospect or client thinks or feels about the product, offering, or service, and might go something like this: "Does a plan like this make sense to take care of your needs and challenges?" Or "Does this plan help you when/solve/earn/achieve/upgrade . . ." Whichever words you choose, these are really simple versions of test closes you can use in your communication with your client. After you use these to discern where in the process the client is, you can proceed to the close, or use a different strategy, if necessary, to keep the discussion open and moving forward.

The **choice close** works well with directors and thinkers. Remember, directors need two choices: for example, "Would the dollar amount you committed to earlier be comfortable, or would this other package pricing be better?" This kind of question gives the control *back* to the director to make the decision, versus the salesperson *telling* them what they "should" do. This is also effective with thinkers, as long as you've already covered the worst-case scenario.

If you can flex the muscles of the **delay close**, the results will blow you away. You can take this approach with prospects or clients of any personality style, and it is best used when you've found yourself in sales jeopardy. Remember: you need to be bold with directors and thinkers, while softening your approach somewhat with feelings-based people. You'll want to use this close when the prospect or client keeps saying "I'm not ready to make the decision," or gives another similar excuse. If you're working with someone who's been delaying for a few weeks—or even up to three or four months—and you're still trying to get them (ridiculous), it's this simple: you call them up. If the person says, "I'm just not ready to do this," you invoke P.S.P, and say, "In my experience, when prospects and clients say they aren't ready to do this, they usually mean "No," but don't want to hurt my feelings by telling me that. I don't suppose that's the case with you, *is it*?" Voice up the end . . . make sure you emphasize the last part of the sentence—and then be quiet. If you've done everything else I've taught you, using this question at this point in the relationship will give you a pure "Yes" or "No" answer. If they say "yes," then congratulations—you're in. If they say "No," that's a good thing as well; you've gotten them off the fence and you're free to take them off your list and begin contacting *other* people who *do* need your product, offer, or service.

What was *my* number-one close when I was in the car business years ago? My favorite close was the **assumptive one**. I found it to be *incredibly* easy. Back in those days, I had a follow-up system for my prospects and clients that included some quirky and fun tactics, so they always knew who I was; these strategies were the actual beginnings of the Marketing Yourself Shamelessly program. They had already seen information from me, typically through referral sources, so I considered it a done deal once they arrived at my office. I assumed the sale because I had earned the right to their business through the steps I had already taken.

There were several tactics that I used besides the T.O.M.A. campaigns. Once a potential client arrived to meet me, I created a picture of them possessing the product in their minds. While standing and talking on the Nissan dealership floor, I used the push-broom paintbrush to convey what the car would look like in their driveway. We talked about what the neighbors would think, where they might take the car on a trip, how the leather seats smelled—all the things connected with car ownership. The prospect's Picasso began to frame the car. After that, it was simple; I just assumed the close. This close still works today—not just on cars, but also on seminars, sales training, and consulting. Anytime I go into a close, I do these things.

The assumptive close can also be called "consent with action." You simply begin to fill out the paperwork and assume the close as it relates to a physical action. For example, let's say that the prospect's last name is Smith. I might say something like, "Perfect. I'll need some basic information to get started. I want to make sure I have the correct spelling of your last name." That's it—even if the last name is something as simple as Smith. This assumed close works most of the time, as long as you do all the work required before it occurs.

The **cushion close** is useful when a client expresses a differing viewpoint or a conflict arises during the final close. Too many salespeople attempt to butt heads and argue; they think that proving the client wrong and themselves right will result in a sale. How do I say this delicately? I can't, so I have to say "No: that just doesn't work." Your reaction should be neutral, nonthreatening, and filled with phrases to diffuse the conflict. Start with simple, positive words like "Okay" and "Great," and then follow through with G.A.R.A. phrases. As soon as you sense this turning point, discontent, or even hostility emerging, use phrases that include "I'm grateful for," "I appreciate that," or "I respect and can agree with you on that." The conflict distracting both you and the client will melt back into the flow of conversation, and you can proceed with the closing.

Smoke-out closes ask "why" in an attempt to identify the real reasons for a client's hesitation. There are four: the direct, the indirect, the bracket, and the isolation. As one would say, be careful when eating fish—you want to remove all the bones before proceeding so that you don't choke. Similarly, you want to remove the objections before proceeding to the close. Don't be so anxious that you miss one objection and choke on it. Simply verify that you have cleared the real objection by countering with a smoke-out question

You will see in the following four closing tactics that I use the word "echo." This means that you restate the client's *exact* protest to them, using the same pitch, pace, and articulation that they used when delivering the message to you. You have to repeat it back to them precisely as they gave it to you.

The *direct smoke-out* is used only when there's a time-related objection. "Would you mind sharing with me why you need to think about this a little bit more?" or "Would you mind sharing with me why you need [echo their specific time limit] to make this decision?"

The *indirect smoke-out* is used with a monetary objection. You might say, "Would you share with me why you think or feel . . ." and echo back the exact money objection they gave you.

The *bracket isolation* is one of my favorite methods, in which you ask "Would you mind sharing with me why . . ." and then echo back what they said, ending with ". . . would prevent you from getting started right now?"

The *isolation* technique is when you say "In addition to . . ." and then echo back their stated objection, continuing with, ". . . is there any *other* reason that would prevent you from starting now?" Again, you won't be able to close until you isolate the objections, eradicate them, and *then* close.

Another closing tactic is (no surprise) using **third party stories**, Fast Facts Profile, Testimonial Sheets, or an actual audio or videotape of a client proclaiming "This product is the greatest thing I've ever purchased!" Third party evidence is always best, since it moves the level of believability into the green zone of the C.B.S. (see Figure 7.1).

Once a client is safely within that green zone, it's time to close. Although members of the financial industry must operate under FINRA regulations and therefore cannot use third party evidence and testimonials, you can state *examples*. When in doubt, always check with your compliance department to be certain.

The final close is the **feel/felt/found**, which is my least favorite. A lot of network-marketing companies across the country recruit people who don't really want to be *sales*people, and this close is exactly what they are taught to use to accomplish a sale. The challenge is that savvy people recognize this as a closing tactic, and usually bust the "salesperson" on it. If you're going to use this close, the rule of thumb is to do so in a warm market scenario—in other words, one in which the potential client really knows you. It works like this: you basically respond to any objection by using phrases like, "I know how you feel," "I felt the same way myself about the product at one point, and then when I did further research (or sat down with the sales manager, or when I tried it myself), I found that it was a dynamic product, solved all my needs, and took care of all my issues." And everybody lived happily ever after.

Although it's effective when used properly, it's a very rudimentary, communication-based closing skill. If it works, great, but there are a lot of network-marketing companies coaching their sales nymphs in this style. These people then infiltrate communities and practice this very close. In fact, some of my students who have used this close have had prospects remark, "I've been to MLM trainings before and I've heard that one." Look both ways before crossing the street with this one, and always use it with a familiar market. Above all, be sincere. If it's based on truth, then you're off to the races.

Now here's your bonus close; you may feel the earth move under your feet on this next one. Again, you've performed all the nuances of the process; you're in discussion with the client and about to land your final approach. Now cue in to the structure of the persuasion: state the prospect's name, enter pause, silence, patience, and then ask, "In your opinion, do you believe this program to be the right thing for you (or your family, company, team, etc.)?" And they will always say "Yes" if you've done the right things. Then you say "Hmm. Tell me something then." (Pause, silence, patience.) *"In all your life, have you ever been sorry for doing the right thing?"* They will always answer "No" to that question. Then immediately tag on the chorus line, "Great. Based on that, let's go ahead and get started with the program/begin filling out the paperwork right now." It's just *that simple*.

We can present our sale in many ways, but handling the situation *after* you hear "No" is where our job really begins, isn't it? *That* is where the rubber meets the road and it's time for you to commit to action. It is vital for you to respond appropriately to earn more sales. Remember this: "Nos" and pushbacks are kissin' cousins in the sales world. My reflex is frequently to acknowledge the comment, ignore it, and then get back to the next step in *my* agenda. Sometimes you have to agreeably fight the word "No." Once upon a time, a long-time sales student and friend of mine named Tom exercised this skill. He created a positive first impression, earned respect, and had done all the right things with his client, yet the client kept saying "No." However, Tom kept going back and engaging the client in more discussion. About 50 minutes into the call, the client *finally* said "Yes"! And it was *not* a beat-up session. They were engaged in a great conversation and both parties had a high level of respect for each other. The fact is that some people simply have made a habit of saying "No." Tom acknowledged the "No," ignored it, and persisted professionally until a successful close came forth. You, too, can overcome a similar situation if you follow Tom's example.

Just as Tom did in his phone call, you have to persist past the first "No," then the second, and then the third. This is similar to peeling back the layers of the onion until you get to the middle. By continuing the conversation, new evidence emerges about why the client or prospect should buy from you. Recently, I engaged in two separate contracts with significant entities here in Dallas. Both parties told me, "We have no budget. We don't want training. We don't *need* training. We're never going to do it." Yet I eventually closed both of them. I ignored their rejections, uncovered their specific wants, needs, and challenges, and was able to provide a solution.

There's an ongoing self-fulfilling prophecy in sales. If you're broke, don't believe in yourself, or walk into your presentation appointment expecting a "No," you'll convey this attitude to everyone present. Some of you make your own worst fears come true; you default to disaster. So don't go telegraphing to the rest of the world that everyone else should be broke just like you and live on Misery Mountain together.

To fill the work boots of a top-ranking producer, you must be a pro with the "No." Don't take this response as a personal rejection. Instead, consider it as a call to action; you can either do the work required to convert it to a "Yes" or confirm it as a true refusal and move on. I have seen salespeople fall to pieces for a day, even for a *week*, over a "No," because—as we discussed previously—they had put such *high hopes* in getting the deal. You have to get "hope" out of your vocabulary and mindset. Success doesn't just happen; opportunity only presents itself when you are proactive. So don't take it personally if you fail to close. If you absolutely need to have a hissy fit, do it for 5 to 30 seconds—and then move on.

And don't fold! Never just say, "Okay. Catch you next time!" When you succumb to that weak response, you devalue all of your previous statements and claims, because you prove it wasn't worth taking another swing. Your attitude determines your profit; you've got the greatest product, offering, or service there ever was, so why would anybody ever say no? Once you are able to let a "No" slide off your back, find some intestinal fortitude with the highest levels of belief in your product, and then respond with "Why would you say 'No' to something that's so awesome?" You may even say, "Our program looks so attractive for you right now; what is your reason for saying 'No'?" (See Figure 2.2.)

Of course you can always doctor your own sales. You're now equipped with the diagnostic psychogenic scorecard, which—as you can see—has 30 points: 10 each for the company, the product/ offer/service, and you. Any time you're above 20 points, there's no F.U.D.; however, anything less than 20 points indicates the presence of Fear, Uncertainty, and Doubt. Everything I have taught you in *Sales Mastery* will raise your score to over 20, and if you work to get to the top of your game, you should be hitting 30 on that scorecard every time you are working with your clients. At this point, you don't even need to ask for the order because your prospects have already become clients and placed the order automatically.

Lastly, don't accept an "uninformed 'No.'" If you are only halfway through your presentation and your client or prospect has already said "No," then politely decline the refusal—tell them "I accept only an *informed* no. The no you are giving me right now is based on the fact that you have not had a full presentation, meaning that you're uninformed." Make sure you provide unabridged information about your product, offering, and service. Show and tell them how it *can* meet their needs and solve their challenges. Stand firm for what you believe in. It always comes back to the faith you have in your product. If they're making an incorrect decision, elegantly let them know that you won't accept it.

Quick Tips for the Closing

- Close according to personality style. There are four different personalities and four different closes; if there is more than one person, you need to close to all types.

- A delayed decision will usually result in a "No" decision; therefore if you get delayed, *do something*.

- *All* decision-makers must be present.
- When a "No" is based on an *uninformed* decision, respectfully decline the refusal.

You can further prevent refusals by taking the Sales S.T.U.D. essential daily vitamin. Make sure to serve up *specific next steps* and dump a lump of *takeaways*; give them something to do or at least to think about. Create anticipation. Have those top-secret mailing campaign programs that do so much good for you with effective follow-up with your clients. Create *urgency* in your sales message. And, last but not least, all communications should be solidly confirmed through a *deadline* using the Outlook calendar invite feature. These things will help make people chase you instead of you chasing them.

The essence of this chapter is revisited in the following sales parody based on the hit TV show *Cops*.

Sales Manager/Cop: (To the sales violator) Sir, step out of the sales floor. I'm gonna need to see your "I don't take "No" from anybody" card and your third party registration.
Salesperson: Well, um, I don't have one.
Sales Manager/Cop: Well, you just accepted an uninformed "No" and folded like a lawn chair in a selling zone. Cruising like that in the "Okay, no problem" gear defeats your purpose and causes wrecks. I am going to have to fine you.
Salesperson: A fine? But I'm broke!
Sales Manager/Cop (ignoring salesperson): We'll just deduct this time-waster ticket from your tiny little paycheck. . . . Now when you pull back onto the sales floor, shift gears and steer into the "Yes" lane. If you just do those little things you've been told, this road will lead you right into the C.B.S. green zone. You'll be all right.

From distinctions and success traits to tie-downs and take-aways, every part of the sales process leads to the closing. The point is to work smarter and to do so in less time. Using sales psychology is a skilled advantage that will assist you in working at the highest levels of sales efficiency. Most importantly, be sure to implement all of the tactical approaches and proven methods that will accelerate your closing curve. The closing process can be an entire waste of your time unless you *work* to become successful at it. (See Figure 10.1.)

FIGURE 10.1

Closing Mastery Commission Development Quiz

Anything fewer than 100 percent correct answers requires immediate additional work!

1. What are the two classes of distinctions that influence your closing success?

2. True or False: Positive or negative, you can transfer your attitude, beliefs, and feelings to a client, even if you don't actually articulate them.

(continued)

(Continued)

3. What do you call a close that paints a picture of ownership for the client?

4. A delayed decision close typically will result in _____. Therefore, if you get delayed, do _____.

5. If anybody tells you "No" based on an uninformed decision, respectfully _____ the "No."

6. Which of these are tie-downs to facilitate closing?
   A. It's a powerful solution, isn't it?
   B. Does that fit into your budget?
   C. Isn't that right?
   D. Don't you agree?

7. What does G.A.R.A. stand for?

8. True or False: Actual closing questions are also yes/no questions.

9. Which of the eight closes could you utilize more often to increase your success rate?

10. Which close works best with directors and thinkers?

(continued)

(Continued)

11. True or False: When you have a client who's been on the fence for a couple of months, but you then readdress their delay and get a "not interested" response, it's best to just take them off your list and begin contacting other people who need your product or service.

12. You won't be able to close until you _____ the objections—there may be more than one.

13. Which close should be used only in a warm market scenario?

14. In Sales Coach Chuck's opinion, what is the most powerful close he's shared?

15. People who stay upset for a prolonged period of time after receiving a "No" are likely to suffer from:
    A. Fast food deprivation
    B. Caffeine withdrawals
    C. Not having a full pipeline
    D. Getting a bad lead

16. Closing starts at the _____ of the sales process.

(continued)

(Continued)

Closing Mastery Quiz Answers

1. Professional *and* personal

2. True

3. Assumptive

4. No, something

5. Decline

6. A, C, and D. Tie-downs will result in "Yes." B is sabotage.

7. Grateful, appreciate, respect, agree

8. False

9. Your answer

10. The choice close

11. False

12. Isolate

13. Feel/Felt/Found

14. In all your life, have you ever been sorry for doing the right thing? Great! Based on that, let's go ahead and start with the payment right now.

15. C

16. Beginning

CHAPTER

11

Don't Procrastinate—Activate!

There are a few things in life that are pure fantasy. The tooth fairy is one of these things, as is the big commission check you think you're going to get as a result of the magical things you think will happen just by reading this book. Sadly, the money isn't just going to start rolling in on its own. You must work diligently and re-dedicate yourself daily to be the sales pro your competition doesn't want to come up against. They're afraid of you, and they should be, because they're going to lose to you. Regardless of rank—whether you're an entry-level sales associate or business owner—this work has to be done. Your own good sense should require you to employ the components of *Sales Mastery*, make them go to work for you, and reap the rewards of your own commitment. Don't just read, or think about what you've read. *Implement* the information. *Activate action!*

In the early 2000s, I taught a one-week Sales Mastery course for a local company. This cycle continued for about 60 months straight at a frequency of four-and-a-half days once a month, with typical enrollment of 20 to 30 people. Approximately 30 percent of the students headed from the course site to their respective homes and started practicing the first active steps to increase their sales first thing Monday morning, if not sooner. The other 70 percent did nothing. They fooled around, or went to Office Depot to buy file folders and Post-it notes and stuff like that, while the 30 percent self-starters were already cranking it out and getting results. You can't sit there and procrastinate on this information; you've got to put it to work immediately. Don't be a member of the 70 percent pack who show up, engage, and do the homework every night, then after all that effort, just five or six days later, are back home ripping open another bag of potato chips while planning to sit on the couch and watch *Desperate Housewives*. That's not going to work. Manage your time and do the work. And unless you want to pay me to be your personal drill sergeant, you're going to have to take some initiatives on your own to move your ace.

Another thing to remember—don't think too much about it. While 30 percent do implement immediately, there's always *some*body who completely overanalyzes the process. Instead of "overdoing the do," he or she overthinks the think—during which he tips his hand to the client or prospect.

A discussion like this can completely contaminate a client visit: "You know, I was just at this Sales Mastery course that this guy named Chuck Bauer taught. He taught us to send stuff to you in a pink envelope without a return address. What are your thoughts on that?" The client's going to respond, "That's kinda peculiar. I don't think I'd like that." The salesperson just talked himself out of doing the work. Don't ask a client's permission to send them material or get in touch with them; that kills the element of surprise. All the effort you made to create anticipation and suspense is spoiled in an instant. A situation like this is simple revenue aversion.

Now listen to the needle scratching the record as I replay your inner thought of "Does this work?" Why waste time wondering? Go do it! We have hundreds upon hundreds of salespeople across the country executing these battle tactics at this very moment. We collect feedback from thousands of them all the time and tweak the methods as we go. Due to this process, Sales Mastery changes every day; it's an ongoing evolution because of the data we're constantly gathering from successful salespeople. So if you still intend to go out and pitch, only to set up that client to talk you out of doing the work, then don't bother with doing anything—because you're going to get spanked by somebody who's been through this course, knows what they're doing, and does it *without revealing their tactics to the client*. Filmmakers like Alfred Hitchcock don't explain the special effects during the course of the movie, do they? They save it for the documentary about the making of the film. In the same way, you don't want to expose your methods to your audience while you're working. Expunge those tactic-explaining pitches and any other unprofessional habit that thwarts a revenue-driven focus. If you don't, you'll only find the reasons to *not* do what you need to do—instead of honing in on the reasons *to do* it.

Those three magic words that I mention early in this book sum up what will help get you started: Discipline, Tenacity, and Implementation. Notice how *none* of these mental cues are "thinking" words; they're words that can only be demonstrated through *activation of action*. You should institute maximum effort towards D.T.I., and on everything on which you've been coached during this course. If your attitude is too casual, you will miss the full extent of the benefits I've described here. These techniques are not to be used separately or randomly; rather, they all work together to harmoniously accomplish the specific goals of Sales Mastery and revenue growth.

The more pressure on the gas pedal, the faster your car goes. The next key concept is fairly simple:

- Mass action = mass results,
- Some action = some results,
- No action = no results.

You have to *work* to accomplish your goals, and the more often and consistently you do those hundreds of little things that make up Sales Mastery, the better the results you will obtain.

I challenge you to do the following within the next 24 hours: Get a legal pad, iPad, computer, or BlackBerry—something you can make notes on—and if you haven't already, begin recording the tips and skills you've learned about in this book that you want to ***activate into action***. And I'll let you know right here: this is not a two-minute task. It should be a 15-minute or longer brain cleanse—dumping everything you knew before and reloading it with what you've gotten out of this book. Creating this void will prompt other, more useful information to pop up in its place. Over the course of the next several days, you'll come up with a thorough agenda based on this book's lessons that will transform your performance from good to great—and from great to *extraordinary!*

You'll remember more than you first thought you would, and then you'll remember even more. Instead of merely breaking any bad habits, you'll replace them with effective ones.

Once you feel that this list is complete, the next step is to prioritize it. Put each focus item into one of the following categories: E for emergent, U for urgent, and NU for nonurgent. Set a deadline for every one of these tasks to insure that you implement them into your sales cycle. The old adage is true: "What gets measured gets done." It's normal to have five to seven items—sometimes more, very rarely less—in each one of the priority categories. Some of you will need to complete tasks as basic as buying envelopes and an accordion folder for your Marketing Yourself Shamelessly campaign. However, you need to establish deadlines even for those mundane chores—which you can do by recording the deadline dates and times in Outlook and holding yourself accountable. *Don't* say to yourself "I'll do it later"—because you won't.

The next step is to take those emergent items—whether it's closing, Marketing Yourself Shamelessly, or taking a specific step—and begin working on them right away. Once you've developed the discipline it takes to become unconsciously competent at the first few items, then you can apply yourself to the second section—the urgent items—and work on those until you're finished. The last thing to work on is the list of nonurgent items—the ones that aren't so critical. Eventually, you will incorporate every one of these tasks seamlessly into your workflow, which will allow you to achieve greater success.

As part of this process, I want you to go to the Resources section in the back of this book, find the link to the GoalMastery Action Plan form that's offered on my website (www.chuckbauer. com/2011_goalplanner/), and access it free of charge. This plan is meant to fully engage the psyche by externalizing your income goal as a derivative of your Sales Mastery knowledge. I'd like to see a six-month sketch expressing what your increase is going to be. The more detailed you make it, the more likely you are to achieve it. If you're averaging $100,000 annually, then we should forecast up to $120,000 or $130,000 in six months as a result of what you've learned in SalesMastery. That's the type of detail you record in the GoalMastery Action Plan form. Brevity, in any form, shows a lack of commitment. I occasionally have sales students who fill out this form very generally and without details—because it's a form and they want to get it back to me as quickly as possible. Guess what? I'm going to be your worst nightmare of a sales coach if you return it to me without any sort of effort or detail, because this shows me that you lack commitment. You need to have an exact plan of what you're going to do.

Here is an example of that. Lee and Michele Odems, of Wood-bridge, Virginia, own a real estate company and were students in my sales management consulting program years ago. I sent them the one-page GoalMastery Action Plan form, and one week later, received a *very* detailed—eight pages long, to be precise—action plan back. It was one of the simplest yet most comprehensive plans that has ever been submitted to me. Those eight pages were full of commitment, thoughts, ideas, and—most importantly—a thorough, meticulous outline for daily, weekly, monthly, and quarterly revenue-producing tasks. The Odems could not miss on their goals, which were written out with the highest levels of commitment and gravity that I've ever seen. Each activating action resulted in another goal: a new home three times larger than the last, a yearly trip to Aruba (always on the same date), followed by a bank account that to this day keeps Lee and Michele smiling. So what about you? Are you going to fill out the one-page form as quickly as possible and turn it back in just to be done? Hmm . . . I wonder.

Allow me to help you with this. A vital part of this exercise is to identify the roadblocks that you can anticipate—so write these down, too. Then identify the actions that will either help you through or will hinder you tackling those roadblocks. Jot down any further education you need, and then visit my website to find a ton of free resources. Maybe some of you need coaching, or to hire me to personally come in and work with your company. Whatever you do, don't leave anything out of your GoalMastery Action Plan.

The engine that drives this plan is your ability to imagine the reward when you hit that income increase. Are you going to Gettysburg with your family, as Jeff Lang did? Or be like Lee and Michele Odems, who enjoy living in an expansive home along with their kids? Whatever reward you choose will motivate you to reach your goal.

If you genuinely want to meet these objectives, you also need to set up an accountability team. There should be at least four people holding you accountable to the goals you've set forth in your Goal-Mastery Action Plan. Do *not* include your spouse or sweetheart on your accountability list. Rather, list people who will be matter-of-fact with you and hold your feet to the fire. Maybe your ex might be better suited to be on your squad. You *can* get that income increase and get *yourself* that well-deserved raise, as long as you remember that it's about *you*—what *you* do, *your* goals, *your* **activation to action**!

Another thing that you can do to maintain a sense of self-accountability is to get a P.M.S. list. (Refer again to the Resource section and find the link to the web page containing the free P.M.S. chart.) I am an aviator, so I also have a P.M.S. (Personal Minimum Standards) list when I fly. I have to hit these Personal Minimum Standards of checking A and doing B before I can expect a safe flight. The same notion applies to your sales process. You first need to determine your daily metrics—those key revenue-producing activities that occur every day, five days a week. I'm not talking about administrative or creative work, and I'm certainly not referring to writing notes about a client in an Outlook contact folder. The work with the potential to trigger a sale is revenue-producing; it's making a call to a client, setting an appointment, following up, and so on. You plug these activities into the P.M.S. tracking system to help you become 10 to 15 percent more efficient. Practicing this psychology in your sales tactics can produce greater yields in an allotted time. Consider this system a method of tracking yourself and your commitment to better performance through your revenue-producing activities. This is a vehicle for measuring real progress—activating through action your awareness of these key *daily* activities to get that 10 percent or more personal raise and increase in your paycheck!

Keep a daily P.M.S. chart, and tally a grade at the end of the week. I suggest that you stretch yourself to make a 90 to 100 percent grade consistently. Now, sales managers, if you are taking a look at this, you can implement this at your company by keeping an eye on the sales students' scores as they're propagated. Saving it an Excel spreadsheet keeps it push-button ready with instructions, so you that can begin implementing it immediately. It goes hand-in-hand with the GoalMastery Action plan, as well as keeping your own metrics tuned into your daily revenue-producing activities.

Go back and look at Jeff Lang. This student of mine was making $250,000 annually and, within six months, gave himself a raise to $385,000. Matt West with Thomson Reuters increased his sales by 40 percent and his income by 35 percent within one year of graduating from the SalesMastery course. In the division of the Fortune 100 that I work with, there has been 40 percent growth rate after the first 12 months. Did this happen by magic? No; it comes down to this: being fully engaged. All my sales students who are highly successful, all my other sales companies, all the business owners with whom I work are *fully engaged*. They accept responsibility for their success without wasting time by assigning blame or justifying. For me and all these other people, this means all or nothing. It's not a 99 percent effort, it's not a 95 percent effort, it's not 90 percent, and it's not 70 percent: it is 100 percent, every single time. So—**how serious are you?** You'll answer that for yourself within the next 24 hours—through your own activation of action, or lack thereof.

Now that you are near the end of this book, I hope you will agree that I have taken great pains to make it a no-bulls—t, real-world tool for your success. But if I may, allow me to take a few of our last moments together to get a bit philosophical (I promise it won't be long!).

Some of my friends and colleagues have asked me why I wrote this book. They know all about my demanding schedule and unbelievable amount of client commitments; they also know that I have sacrificed a good chunk of change on the hours I spent writing the little labor of love you hold in your hands. They know how hard I have worked on writing, rewriting, and rewriting yet again section after section in an effort to make sure it serves you. Why do all this? Here's why: after more than 26 years as a successful sales pro, sales trainer, sales consultant, and sales coach, and after seeing so much garbage out there in the sales training marketplace, I simply felt that I had to take a stand.

Don't get me wrong. While I have a healthy ego, I am not stupid enough to believe that mine is the last word on sales effectiveness. There are some good trainers out there who are teaching quality information. The sad fact of the matter is, however, that these good trainers are unfortunately few and far between; the vast majority of what I see being passed off as solid sales training could fertilize the Mojave Desert. And, frankly, that gets my dander up.

You see, I don't only consider sales to be an honorable profession, or even a noble calling. I literally see it as the thing *that makes the world work* the way it was created to work. There is a common saying that nothing happens until someone sells something, and as true as that statement is, I still don't believe that most of the people who say it truly understand the gravity of that statement. Selling isn't just the linchpin of the business world; it is central to who we are as human beings. Think about it: every human interaction is ultimately an exchange of value, hopefully for the mutual benefit of both parties. To the extent that we become better at these transactions, humankind becomes better, period. So to the extent that I help you become better at sales, I help make the world better for all of us. Call me crazy, but that's what I believe.

So I decided to write this book to share with people everywhere who are serious about making a difference for themselves, their families, and their customers and clients, to make available the tools and techniques to allow them to do so. You now have the proven, precious road map to sales success right in front of you. (See Figure 11.1.) The only question left is, "What are you going to do with it?"

FIGURE 11.1

You are either fully engaged or you are completely disengaged. If you act at the highest levels of Discipline, Tenacity, and Implementation, quite frankly, the world is yours. It doesn't matter what your specific sales job or situation is; you've got all the tools in this book to help you become more successful and more gratified on payday. So upon your next step towards greater rewards, I wish you Godspeed in your goal attainment and your sales career. The information I have shared with you *will* make a difference for you, professionally as well as personally. Don't procrastinate! Activate—right now!

Don't Procrastinate—Activate! Commission Development Quiz

Anything fewer than 100 percent correct answers requires immediate additional work!

Answer True or False for each of the following statements:
1. Thoroughly analyze a tactic before implementing it to insure its success.

(*continued*)

(*Continued*)

2. Always check with one of your top clients before implementing any new marketing or follow-up processes to get some live preliminary feedback.

3. The three "thinking" words to keep your sales wheels rolling are discipline, tenacity, and implementation.

4. Mass action = mass results, some action = working smarter, and no action = no results.

5. Classifying tasks as emergent, urgent, or nonurgent nullifies the need to set an actual deadline for these tasks.

6. As long as you identify your main objective while goal-setting, the details aren't as important.

7. It's also a waste of time when setting goals to give thought to possible roadblocks to that goal, because life is unpredictable.

8. A worthwhile reward for hitting my income goal is to pay another bill.

9. I should ask my sweetheart to help hold me accountable since these goals will affect us both, and because it's convenient that we're around each other so much.

(*continued*)

(Continued)

10. Now that I've got a P.M.S. chart, I can record how truly busy I am with my administrative work . . . because the more of that I do, the more revenue-producing I'll actually be.

11. I can do all of this later, especially since there's a new episode of *Desperate Housewives* on right now.

Don't Procrastinate—Activate! Quiz Answers

1. False

2. False

3. False—these are *action* words!

4. False—some action = some results

5. False

6. False

7. False

8. False

9. False

10. False

11. False—don't procrastinate, activate!

Resources

Chuck Bauer's Website: www.chuckbauer.com

Sales Tools Website: www.cbsalestools.com

Sales Tools Menu Page: www.cbsalestools.com/sales-tools/

Free Sales Training Videos and Articles: www.chuckbauer.com/videos.articles/

Fast Start for Your Sales—Free Sales Tools: www. chuckbauer .com/faststart

Secondary T.O.M.A. Campaign (S.T.C.): www.chuckbauer.com/stc

Books

Positive First Impression Books by Jim Rohn: www.cbsalestools .com/sales-tools/top-secret-positive-first-impression-books/

Chuck Bauer SalesMastery Book of Quotes: http://www.cbsalestools .com/sales-tools/salesmastery-book-of-quotes/

Sales Mastery by Chuck Bauer, published by John Wiley & Sons: www.chuckbauer.com/salesmasterybook

Follow Sales Coach Chuck!

Facebook: www.facebook.com/SalesCoachChuck
Twitter: http://twitter.com/coachchuckbauer
YouTube: www.youtube.com/user/getsalesresultsnow
LinkedIn: www.linkedin.com/in/chuckbauer

Low Cost, High Quality Printing: www.pfl.com/salescoachchuck

Colored Envelopes: www.paperworks.com

Nido Qubein: www.nidoqubein.com

Video and Audio E-Mail: www.chuckbauer.com/video

Goal Action Plan Form: www.chuckbauer.com/PDF/GoalMastery _Action_Plan.pdf

P.M.S.—Personal Minimum Standards: www.chuckbauer.com/ pms

Chuck's Client List: www.chuckbauer.com/clients/

Testimonials: www.chuckbauer.com/testimonials/

Seminars and Workshops: www.chuckbauer.com/sales-seminars/

Consulting: www.chuckbauer.com/sales-training-consulting/

Recommended Books

The 4-Hour Work Week by Timothy Ferriss
How to Win Friends & Influence People by Dale Carnegie
Management Rewired by Charles S. Jacobs
Microsoft Outlook 2007 Plain & Simple by Jim Boyce
Microsoft Outlook 2010 Plain & Simple by Jim Boyce
Words That Sell by Richard Bayan

Chuck's Crazy Acronyms (C.C.A.)

A.B.F.	Awesome Bass Fisherman
B.R.P.P.	Buyers Remorse Prevention Package (Pronounced BURP)
C.B.S.	Clients Believability Scale
C.O.K.	Cups of Knowledge
D.S.R.T.	Director, Relater, Socializer, Thinker
D.T.I.	Discipline, Tenacity, Implementation
E.	Emergent
E.S.C.	Emergent Sales Challenge
E.T.A.	Estimated Time of Accomplishment
F.F.P.	Fast Facts Profile
F.H.A.	Fog, Haze, Ambiguity
F.O.N.	Freak of Nature (top 3 percent of all salespeople)
F/U	Follow Up
F.U.D.	Fear, Uncertainty, Doubt
G.A.R.A.	Grateful, Appreciate, Respect, Agree
H.E.	Happy Ears
H.S.D.	Hear, See, Do!
I.H.C.	Intimate Human Connection
K.O.D.	Kiss of Death
L	Lazy
L.O.R.	Lack of Respect
L.R.S.	Listenable Rate of Speech
M.O.O.	Method of Operation
M.P.C.	Main Point Card
M.V.A.	Most Valuable Advocate
NU	Nonurgent
N.R.P.A.	Nonrevenue-Producing Activity
O.O.	Overcoming Objections
O.O.S.S.	Overcoming Objection Sales Sheet
P.D.R.	Practice, Drill, Rehearse
P-D-R	Plan–Do–Review
P.M.S.	Personal Minimum Standards

P.O.S.	Product, Offering, Service
P.S.P.	Pause, Silence, Patience
R.P.A.	Revenue-Producing Activity
R.R.C.	Referral Response Card
R.R.P.	Referral Response Program
R.T.	Roger That
S.A.T.	Shock & Awe Tactic
S.C.C.B.	Sales Coach Chuck Bauer
S.S.P.	Standard Sales Pitch
S.T.C.	Secondary TOMA Campaign
S.T.P.	Sales Tune-Up
S.T.U.D.	Specific Next Step, Takeaway, Urgency, Deadline
S.W.	Sales Weenie
T.I.P.S.	To Insure Prompt Sales
T.O.M.A.	Top Of Mind Awareness
T.S.M.C.	Top Secret Mailing Campaign
P.V.S.	Professional Visitor Syndrome
P.V.	Professional Visitor
P.C.	Professional Closer
U	Urgent
U.A.	Urban Advisor
V.U.	Voice Up
W	Whatever
W	Winner
W	Welcome
W.C.S.	Worst-Case Scenario
W.G.M.G.D.	What Gets Measured Gets Done
W.I.R.	Week in Review
W.S.D.	World Sales Domination
W.T.D.	Write This Down
10.4	Acknowledged

Index